D1383986

PIGEON
RIVER
COUNTRY
The Big Wild

by

Gordon Charles

To Jude & Dale:
With all best wishes,
Gordon Charles

WILLIAM B. EERDMANS PUBLISHING COMPANY
GRAND RAPIDS, MICHIGAN

Dedicated to Ford Kellum and the other "little people" who believed enough in the Pigeon River Country to fight for it with their time, talents, and dollars to save it from destruction.

CONTENTS

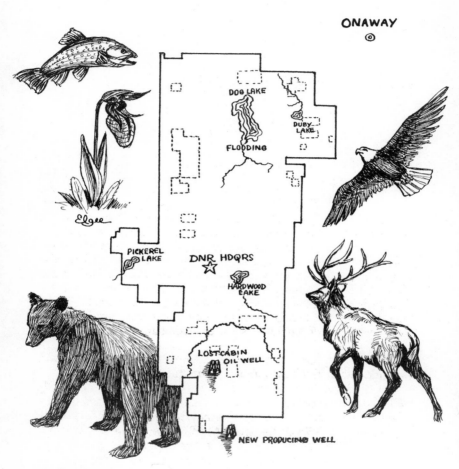

◎ **INDIAN RIVER**

ONAWAY
◎

DOG LAKE

DUBY LAKE

FLOODING

PICKEREL LAKE

DNR HDQRS ☆

HARDWOOD LAKE

LOST CABIN OIL WELL

NEW PRODUCING WELL

Elgee

◎ **GAYLORD**

ATLANTA ◎

The Pigeon River Country is located near the northern tip of Michigan's lower peninsula, some forty miles south and east of the Straits of Mackinac. It includes parts of Cheboygan, Otsego, and Montmorency counties (see map, p. 70).

Foreword

The date is one I'll never forget.

It was July 2, 1970. I was driving the nearly two hundred miles from my northern Michigan home to Lansing on a sad mission. My good friend and associate James L. Rouman, executive director of Michigan United Conservation Clubs (MUCC), had died two days earlier, and I wanted to attend his funeral.

Near Clare I turned on the car radio for the morning news, and when I heard it a shudder of revulsion ran through me. The big story of the day concerned a major oil and gas find in the Pigeon River Country, just off the Lost Cabin Trail. The Shell Oil Company had made a big strike at the Charlton #1-4 site the day before. Predictions were rampant that much of the northern part of Michigan's lower peninsula was sitting on a vast oil field.

You really have to know the Pigeon River Country to have any idea what that could mean for its future.

Consisting of roughly five hundred square miles of mostly wild lands, at least forty percent of it is owned by the state. It's ninety-five percent recreational land, bounded on all four sides by highways—I-75 to the west, M-68 to the north, M-33 to the east, and M-32 to the south. Communities closest to the four corners are Gaylord, Indian River, Onaway, and Atlanta.

Almost all of the upstream watersheds for the Pigeon, Sturgeon, and Black Rivers are contained within the land's forest, all three of which could and should qualify for designation as national wild rivers.

A rolling topography supporting young, vigorous hardwoods and coniferous swamps borders the three main streams. The terrain is vital to wildlife, especially during Michigan's severe deep-snow winters.

Primitive, "no-frills" camping is available in several campgrounds in the Pigeon River Country.

Within the Pigeon River Country are a half-dozen forest campgrounds, most of which are located on the area's unspoiled lakes and rivers. A motorist can travel twenty miles in any direction without seeing a house, cottage, fence, or anything else manmade. There is no other place in Michigan's lower peninsula like it.

Large enough to absorb a reasonable number of visitors, the area provides opportunities for a variety of outdoor recreational activities. Many people enjoy just driving the two-track trails to take in the incredible scenery and capture it on film. Fishing, hunting, camping, swimming, boating, and horseback riding on the fine trail system are also very popular. And the area's five hundred square miles are also able to support private harvesting of wild berries and mushrooms as well as commercial harvesting of the bulk of northern Michigan's forest products.

Perhaps highest on the list of the area's fascinating features is the roster of creatures that makes up its wildlife community. The largest herd of wild elk east of the Mississippi lives in the rather limited confines of the Pigeon River Country, along with black bears, bobcats, bald eagles, ospreys, pileated woodpeckers, and ravens, all of which are considered fairly rare south of the Straits of Mackinac. Such species require large tracts of wild, quiet habitat, free from the harassment of "civilization" during much of the year. Without such natural protection, their numbers tend to dwindle as breeding habits are repeatedly interrupted.

At the time of the Shell Oil strike, the Pigeon River Country was made up of portions of three smaller state forests, all managed by the state's Department of Natural Resources. There weren't that many conflicts among the groups using the area because the DNR was doing a good job of screening out groups that it thought might prove harmful.

It was only because DNR officials in Lansing felt there wasn't even a remote chance that oil or gas might be discovered in the area that they granted leases on the state land. The lease money looked good, and they considered the risks to be virtually nonexistent.

They were wrong.

How bitterly ironic that Jim Rouman, the man who spearheaded MUCC's famous drive to save the Porcupine Mountains Wilderness State Park from exploitation by timber and mineral interests, should die just one day before Michigan's most valuable state-owned wild lands were discovered to contain the sort of riches that would attract corporations only too willing to rape the north country to get them!

Nor did anyone suspect that without Rouman's able leadership, MUCC would eventually join in with the oil industry and the Michigan DNR to seek further drilling in the Pigeon River Country.

Against such an imposing array of wealth, power, and strength, though, there did arise one man who swore to protect the Pigeon River Country, however hopeless the odds might have seemed: Ford Kellum.

Ford Kellum at temporary Lost Cabin Trail sign.

1

FORD KELLUM

"First they took everything off the top of the ground. Now they're going to take everything from under the ground!"

That was how Ford Kellum reacted as he visited a new oil field in southeastern Antrim County in northern Lower Michigan early in 1969.

He displayed a photograph he had taken in the Deward area. There was a huge oil derrick towering over an expanse of ancient white pine stumps. In the foreground was a sign erected by the state DNR dedicating it as the nation's first "Pine Stump Preserve."

The sign had been placed there only after years of hard work by Kellum, who had at the time been wildlife biologist for the DNR in the Traverse City district. Believing that present and future generations should be aware of what had happened to Michigan's vast pine forests as a result of the uncontrolled logging that took place during the late nineteenth and early twentieth centuries, Kellum had whipped up public support and eventually managed to get fifty-five acres of the best-preserved white pine stumps dedicated as a rare showpiece of the past.

Kellum was himself a rarity among DNR employees. His formal education had stopped at high school. He had no college degree when he joined the Michigan Department of Conservation (the forerunner of the state's DNR) in 1933, becoming a fire towerman and then fire warden at Baldwin.

He transferred to the Cusino Wildlife Experiment Station at Shingleton in 1937 to work with deer and moose in huge

1

The peace and quiet of Michigan's first "Pine Stump Preserve" was destroyed by an oil rig right on its edge. PHOTO COURTESY OF FORD KELLUM

wooded corrals that were designed to be as natural as possible. It became the only place in the world where moose were bred and raised in captivity. The Station also raised a few captive bears, wolves, and blue grouse from Montana, although later releases of the birds were never successful. Kellum published his research findings in a special pamphlet for his employers in Lansing.

A year later Kellum successfully completed an examination and achieved the rank of Biologist I. His salary went from $105 to $155 a month while he was at Cusino. Eventually he transferred to the Iosco Game Refuge in the lower peninsula, then to Crystal Falls back up in the upper peninsula, then back down to Mio, and then, in 1947, to Traverse City, where he served as the district game supervisor.

The fact that he had no college education never bothered Kellum a bit. It surely didn't stop him from having an avid interest in reading and an insatiable curiosity about all living things. In Traverse City he quickly became a close friend of Harold Titus, longtime conservation editor of *Field and Stream* and author of many books, including *The Land Nobody Wanted*, which describes the rape of Michigan's vast forest lands.

When the Great Depression arrived in Michigan, huge tracts of land that had been laid bare by indiscriminate timber harvesting and then abandoned came into the state's hands when the owners couldn't pay the taxes on them. Nobody really felt they were worth keeping anyway. But as time passed, an amazing thing happened. Nature began to fill in many of the openings left by the loggers and the wild fires that had followed them. Trees began to grow again and soon the forests began to return. In some areas, such as Deward, where sterile soils kept growth to a minimum, sharptailed grouse prospered in the openings between the ancient pine stumps.

Kellum and his fellow wildlife biologists had a hard time trying to prevent ambitious DNR foresters from planting all of the openings with pine seedlings, which would have doomed the wildlife that depended on the open habitats. The pine stump preserve in the Deward area was one of the few open spaces that was kept unplanted — although oil and gas discoveries were soon to pose another threat to the wildlife growing there.

Portions of southern Michigan have long yielded up large quantities of oil and gas, but periodic exploration in the north had turned up little or nothing. When the petroleum industry began to ask for leases in the northern counties on state-owned lands, the DNR had no inkling that anything substantial would develop.

Thus, as one state official put it, when several million acres of state land were leased to the oil companies during the late sixties, often for as little as three dollars an acre, "It looked like an easy source of money for the DNR. We never dreamed anything would come of the leases."

But of course something did come of them. Seismic exploration indicated deposits in a donut-shaped formation that was once the shoreline of an ancient lake bed. The northern edge of what was called the Niagaran Reef formation ran squarely through the Pigeon River Country.

The DNR looked to be stuck with the worst end of a bad bargain, but all the people of Michigan were set to bear the loss.

Foresight is a rare trait, but fortunately Ford Kellum had it. During his tenure as biologist in the Traverse City district, he was responsible for an area that included the Dead Stream Swamp in Missaukee and Roscommon counties. Oil and gas had been discovered there some years before, and the results gave him a practical education in exactly what kind of impact exploration and development could have on a once-wild area.

The big swamp had been cut into a checkerboard of trails, pipelines, and rights-of-way that nearly destroyed the entire area. From the air it resembled a giant tic-tac-toe. Long scars slashed through the woodlands, and a three-acre drilling site spread out from the center of each square.

All the roads provided easy access for hunters, trappers, and other recreation-seekers to the entire swamp and the surrounding country, and they weren't long in moving in. In a shockingly short amount of time Dead Stream Swamp's large population of bears, bobcats, and other sensitive species were reduced to near extinction. Even a complete ban on bear and bobcat hunting did little to protect their numbers. Pressures on their habitats from large numbers of sightseers made survival difficult.

Kellum's stay in Traverse City ended in 1964, when the DNR district office was moved to Cadillac as part of a reorganization. Rather than accepting the assignment to the Cadillac post, Kellum asked to be sent to the DNR's Gaylord district. Their decision to grant his request was to haunt his superiors in the years to come. It put him squarely in the middle of the Pigeon River Country drama when the oil strike was made years later.

During his period of service in the Traverse City district, Kellum had been instrumental in organizing the Walter Hastings Audubon Club, so named for an early naturalist and wildlife photographer with the old Department of Conservation. Kellum became the club's first president and helped make it the most active such organization in the state.

Twelve years later, after he had moved to the Gaylord district, he gathered together enough interested individuals to form the Pigeon River Audubon Club. He sensed that there would soon be a need for help to defend the north country against growing commercial exploitation.

Ford Kellum pauses to pay tribute to P. S. Lovejoy, founder of the Pigeon River Country. A simple stone monument was placed in a beauty spot after Lovejoy's ashes were scattered nearby to give him a permanent resting place in the spot he loved best.

2
P. S. LOVEJOY

Among the men Ford Kellum most admired during his years in the Department of Conservation was Parish Storrs ("P. S.") Lovejoy, who is credited with originally creating what he called the "Big Wild"—the Pigeon River Country. When Kellum moved to the Gaylord district, and into close proximity to the Pigeon River Country, he found even more reason to fight for the traditions maintained by Lovejoy.

"P. S. Lovejoy was Michigan's version of, and contemporary of, Aldo Leopold," says Dr. Rupert Cutler, himself a nationally recognized activist in the wilderness movement. (Then serving as assistant U.S. secretary of agriculture, Cutler later joined the national staff of the Audubon Society.)

In a career much like Leopold's, Lovejoy studied forestry, worked for five years as a forest supervisor for the U.S. Forest Service, taught forestry at the University of Michigan, and finally became administrator of the Michigan Department of Conservation.

Among Lovejoy's many accomplishments were the organization and administration of Michigan's Land-Economic Survey, which kept track of how more than seven million acres of wildland were being used. He also created the department's game, fire control, and lands divisions as well as the Institute for Fisheries Research. He also dedicated himself to the development of Michigan's first wildlife refuges and public hunting grounds, including what became the Pigeon River Country.

P. S. exercised the broad authority delegated to him by the

director of the Conservation Department, P. J. Hoffmaster. In 1919 he began the drive to enlarge the state's holdings around the Pigeon River Country. It originally consisted of 6,468 acres of tax-reverted lands in northeastern Otsego County and the 13,320 acres of the Otsego Wildlife Refuge east of Vanderbilt, which had been purchased mostly with hunting license revenues.

In 1918 and 1919, seven Rocky Mountain elk were released in the cutover forest lands in an attempt to reestablish a wild elk population in Michigan, where they had once been native. Years later, these elk were to become the focal point of the battle to save the Pigeon River Country.

Papers he left behind when he died in 1942 show that Lovejoy was almost totally preoccupied with his "Pigeon River Project" during the early 1930s. His vision for what was then just some scrubby northern Michigan lands was an inspiring one.

As Cutler has pointed out, Lovejoy's enthusiasm about the Big Wild had the flavor of Bob Marshall's expressions of deep affection for the Adirondacks, now a "forever wild" state park, and of Sig Olson's hymns to the beauty of the Quetico-Superior voyageur country, now called the Boundary Water Canoe Area.

Lovejoy referred to the Pigeon River Country as "the Wilderness Tract" or "the P. R." "The essence of our proper job on the P. R.," he wrote, "is to handle, so 10-25-50 years hence, the then people of the sort which count most will not be cussing us; will mebbe be saying 'Good Eye.' "

It was his first concern to "handle so as to conserve (prevent bumming up of) the peculiar resources and facilities inherent in that sort of land and water," he wrote, and that was going to involve establishing "permanent and public ownership" and preserving the "flavor and feel of the Big Wild."

Explaining the importance of public ownership, he wrote that "We should not all try for (or permit) such developments or use as is already amply available and as will continue available to the general public . . . because there is chance and occasion to provide something much wanted (needed) and not otherwise readily available to the public.

"Don't we all want, yen for, need, some considerable 'getting away' from the crowds and the lawn mowers and the tulips? (Or enough of us to make the fraction worth catering to?) Isn't that the yen for the Big Wild feel and flavor? I claim it is.

"Therefore, I claim that anything which jeopardizes the [Big Wild feel and flavor] of the Pigeon River et al. (refuges, state

8

forests, etc.) is all wrong—poison! Highways and trails . . . and parked-up campsites are jeopardizing the peculiar resources and facilities of our wild-land tracts (of which the Pigeon River is the biggest and the best).

"I'd like to see the Pigeon opened up to insure really good fire protection and damn little more . . . so that it isn't too damn easy for the beer-belly gents and the nice old grandmaws to get to, set on and leave their tin cans at. I figger that a whole lot of the side-road country should be left plenty bumpy and bushy and some so you go in on foot—or don't go at all."

Even in death, P. S. Lovejoy didn't leave his beloved Pigeon River Country. His will instructed that his ashes be scattered over the area. A plaque fixed to a huge native boulder serves as a visible reminder of his importance in creating the area.

3

SOUNDING THE ALARM

As a defender of the P. S. Lovejoy tradition, Ford Kellum began to sound the alarm in the mid-sixties. He told anybody who'd listen that the oil drillers who were just then starting to head north would inevitably upset the forest ecology and destroy the area's wilderness aesthetic.

Only a few reporters from the northern newspapers were willing to help spread the word. Among the papers that did help press the cause were *The North Woods Call* in Charlevoix, the *Otsego County Herald-Times* in Gaylord, and the *Traverse City Record-Eagle*. The public for the most part remained uninterested.

Nor did Kellum get any help from DNR officials. The Department's director, Ralph A. MacMullan, and its geology chief, Gerald Eddy, both insisted that Michigan's oil industry had an "unblemished record." They told Kellum he had no evidence to support his claims that the activities of the oil companies would endanger the wildlife or spoil the natural beauty of the north country.

Field foresters, biologists, and researchers provided the only professional support for Kellum's cause—and most of the those who were qualified to comment on the facts of the case were unwilling to put their careers on the line to challenge the DNR's top brass. In the end, Kellum often stood alone on the issue, stubbornly refusing to follow orders from Lansing to sign drilling permits for wilderness areas.

On February 19, 1970, the Pigeon River Audubon Club unanimously approved a resolution drafted by Kellum that asked for a ban on all oil drilling in the Pigeon River Country. The Thunder Bay Audubon Club and the Michigan Bear Hunters Association also gave the measure full support.

Just two weeks after the Pigeon River Audubon Club approved Kellum's resolution there was a huge gas well explosion at a drilling site on state land south of Gaylord. It burned out of control until a crew of fire fighters from Texas, led by the famed Red Adair, were called in to put it out. Fortunately, snow on the ground minimized damage to the area from the blaze. If it had happened during the tinder-dry summer season, the results could easily have been catastrophic. To Ford Kellum and his growing number of followers it was an early sign of what could follow if drilling were permitted in the Pigeon River Country.

News of the spectacular gas well fire managed to impress others as well. The Michigan legislature hastily passed a resolution demanding that the DNR call off a pending oil lease sale that would have opened up another 59,000 acres of state-owned land for oil and gas exploration until the public could be given a chance to have its say on the matter.

In late April of 1970, Kellum counted six sharptailed grouse performing their traditional springtime dance near an operating oil well in southern Otsego County. He noted that it was difficult to hear the birds over the noise of the pumps. The following day he observed eleven sharptails near Lake of the North, a seventeen-square-mile land development in northern Antrim County not far south of Gaylord. Within two years all of the birds from both flocks had disappeared because of the constant human disturbance in the areas.

May 1970 found Kellum and other field men from the Gaylord DNR district office opposing an application from Shell Oil Company to sink a well in a deer yarding area just off the Lost Cabin Road. The area was so wild that it was commonly used by the DNR as a release site for nuisance bears. Elk and pileated woodpeckers had also found a haven there.

Kellum made use of every opportunity to speak out about his concerns for the area. On May 6 he wrote the following in the *Otsego County Herald-Times*:

"We have all been progressing ourselves right up to a calamity ever since the Pilgrims landed on Plymouth Rock in 1620. People have been fighting nature—not living with it. We have been taking from our natural resources and put nothing back.

"We promote more and more tourists to deface our North

11

Scenic vistas such as this one are to be found in many parts of the Pigeon River Country.

Bull elk with his harem of cows in the early morning fog.
PHOTO COURTESY OF FORD KELLUM

Country, pollute our waters, spoiling that which they came to enjoy. More promotion and more highways. Is this progress? Or would progress be less promoting and abandoning a highway or two?

"Our tax base will have to be adjusted. Let's not tax our wild and aesthetic lands or marshes so high that the owner will be forced to sell to a land developer, ruining the area for what it was best suited. Along with an adjusted tax base, how about city, county, or state guidelines for all land users and zoning?

"More of man's waste, as well as the waters and soils must be recycled and used again. This would be real progress.

"SUMMARY: Too many people is our number one problem. Reverse the population growth, then most other environmental problems become secondary. Waste less. Buy wisely and reuse many times anything we can. Respect our soil, air and water. Live in harmony with nature. Educate ourselves, beautify and enjoy living. That's progress."

On May 12, 1970, Kellum met with DNR assistant director Gene Gazlay and told him that he could not approve any drilling in the Pigeon River Country despite the fact that leases had already been sold to the oil companies. Gazlay, who had received some of his early training as a game biologist under Kellum, was sympathetic and promised to work for a new policy, but he said that the DNR was "duty bound" to allow drilling and he hoped that Kellum would change his mind.

Two days later, Kellum went to the Lost Cabin Trail along with Troy Yoder, Roger Rasmussen, John MacGregor, Steve Swan, Ralph King, Jerry Lawrence, and DNR deputy director Warren Shapton. The eight DNR men had to make a decision.

At the proposed site of the Charlton #1-4 oil well, Kellum said he would not approve any drilling permit request because of potential harm to wildlife at the location, right on the edge of the Black River Swamp. The vote was five to three to allow drilling by Shell Oil, with Kellum, Swan, and King casting the opposing votes. Kellum told Shapton that if the well turned out to be a producer, he would retire from the DNR and fight "as long as I can to protect the Pigeon River Country."

Late that same May, Gazlay and some others from the Lansing DNR office came up north at Kellum's invitation and toured the Lake of the North and Wilderness Valley land developments. Gazlay expressed shock at what he agreed was the "growing rape of the north country" and took notes that prompted DNR director MacMullan to make a similar tour later on in the summer of 1970.

Kellum's tour continued up the Lost Cabin Trail to where the oil derrick for the Charlton #1-4 drilling site stood. Gazlay admitted that it had been a mistake to allow exploration in that spot. Pressing his advantage, Kellum told him that field men had never had a chance to pass judgment on drilling sites — all such decisions were made in the Roscommon and Lansing offices of the DNR. Gazlay promised that henceforth field men would have the first chance to decide on oil well locations.

On June 25 Kellum and his field men accompanied two DNR geologists to the Elk Hill Trail Camp area. Wildlife, forestry, and fisheries representatives had already said that no drilling should be permitted in the area, but a geologist had said, "We'll put this well right down by the Pigeon River if we want to!" As it turned out, a well was eventually sunk in the area, but it turned up dry, a fact that left the field men grinning broadly.

As time went on, a rift continued to grow between the DNR's field men and their superiors in Roscommon and Lansing. The officials dismissed the field men as "uninformed" and indicated that they intended to make only token concessions to soothe the public protests that were beginning to build in volume. By the summer of 1970, more than 600,000 acres of state lands had been leased to oil and gas firms.

But even the DNR officials sensed some danger in the situation. They agreed to prohibit oil drilling within a quarter of a mile of designated trout streams. They knew that an oil spill into the pristine waters of the Pigeon River Country would spark an immediate public outcry.

But the geologists were less cautious. They continued to oppose the efforts of the field men, arguing that state law "does not give natural resources managers any right to object to the location of oil wells on the grounds that wildlife and fish habitats and aesthetics will be destroyed." They also maintained that oil wells were a "tourist attraction" that should be welcomed by nearby chambers of commerce. And they told the field men that their only responsibility as far as oil exploration was concerned was to determine the value of the timber that would have to be destroyed in order to build roads and lay pipelines to the new oil well sites.

The pure waters of the area are admirably suited for fisheries research.

The Pigeon River is an excellent trout stream.

4

THE BLACKEST OF DAYS

For Ford Kellum and many others throughout Michigan, July 1, 1970, was among the blackest of days. That was the day Shell Oil announced a major oil strike at its Charlton #1-4 site on the Lost Cabin Trail, a two-track path near the Pigeon River Research Station. It was exactly what the DNR field men had long feared most and fought so hard to prevent.

The oil strike was indeed rich. One private property owner in the area who had to that point refused to lease his lands to the oil companies was now offered $50,000 cash for a lease on his forty-acre tract. Nearly everything else in the area, both state and private holdings, had already been leased. Many of the local people were dazzled by thoughts of sudden riches.

It came as quite a blow to Kellum, but he didn't give up. Instead, he set his jaw a little harder, met with some of his followers, and mapped a new strategy. With the help of *The North Woods Call* and the *Otsego County Herald-Times*, they launched a petition drive designed to force the DNR to hold a public hearing on oil well placement in the Pigeon River Country.

In response to pressure from the public, the DNR did agree to hold one hearing in Lansing on July 23 and another hearing at a place and time to be decided later. The aim of those opposed to the drilling was to overturn the siting regulations that were in effect at the time, which allowed one well per forty-acre parcel. Under such rules, the Pigeon River Country might well be cut up into a series of small blocks like the Dead Stream Swamp farther south—with similarly damaging results. A "checkerboard" treatment would destroy the identity of P. S. Lovejoy's beloved Big Wild for all time.

Those who attended the hearings, both of which were chaired by the DNR's state supervisor of wells, Gerald Eddy, found it hard to believe what happened. Eddy's hearing committee was made up of members of the Oil Advisory Board—a group composed entirely of representatives of the oil companies that were leasing lands in the Pigeon River Country and other portions of northern Lower Michigan.

Testimony from 150 people was presented at the second hearing, which was eventually held in Gaylord, but the ruling Eddy handed down less than a week later indicates that he wasn't much swayed by it. He announced that the oil companies would be allowed to drill eight wells per square mile—one well in every eighty acre tract—within the Pigeon River Country. After declaring that he had not "lost a case in thirty years," Eddy added adamantly that "If we don't adopt eighty-acre spacing, we will automatically revert to forty-acre spacing." For all intents and purposes the oil firms were left free to drill at sites of their own choosing in the Pigeon River Country where they held leases.

Drilling was expected to be most extensive in a sixteen-square-mile tract in the southern portion of the Pigeon River Country in Otsego County that was under lease to Shell Oil, Pan-American Petroleum, and Northern Michigan Exploration, a subsidiary of Consumers Power Company of Michigan. Shell held fifty percent of the leases.

During the months that followed, Lost Cabin Trail changed from a two-track path to a fifty-foot-wide bulldozed road capable of handling heavy traffic at high speeds through the forest. It seemed likely that other wild areas would soon enough be opened up with similar roadways leading to sites where the oil companies wanted to drill.

While the oil companies were raising dust in northern Michigan during July of 1970, the state legislature was passing HB-3055 in Lansing. It was a light of hope for the future.

Formally known as the Michigan Environmental Protection Act (MEPA), HB-3055 was designed to give citizens the right to sue both polluters and governmental agencies that were negligent in preventing pollution. Those who backed MEPA, including its brilliant author, Dr. Joseph L. Sax of the University of Michigan law school, suspected that it could also be successfully used to stop the ruination of wilderness areas and the de-

Lost Cabin Trail, once a charming little two-track, was widened and "improved" for high-speed truck traffic by oil producers.

struction of wildlife species. It became effective on October 1, 1970, three months after it was signed into law by Governor William G. Milliken, who had backed it strongly.

Lansing lawmakers also responded to growing public outrage at what was happening in the Pigeon River Country by putting pressure on the state's Natural Resources Commission. (The Commission is the legal, policy-making body of the DNR. It is composed of seven private citizens working without pay for what they regard as the all-important goal of protecting the state's vital outdoor resources.) Under the leadership of commissioner Carl T. Johnson of Cadillac, who went out on his own to investigate drilling practices, that body agreed to suspend all further lease sales until January 1, 1971.

In early August of 1970, field personnel at the DNR's Gaylord district office were ordered to "zone" all portions of their district in which restrictions on use should be imposed. They were given less than two weeks to complete a task that according to Kellum should have taken at least a year, but they buckled down and tackled the job.

All lands had to be placed in one of the following categories: (1) areas in which there should be no oil leasing, construction of pipelines or power lines, road building, or other development; (2) areas in which there should be only limited or restricted development; (3) areas in which there could be certain types of development, such as the creation of snowmobile trails, but in which there should be no oil well drilling; or (4) areas that were already so heavily developed or so close to being developed that further oil drilling, road building, and the like would do little additional harm.

Meanwhile, Otsego County's Board of Commissioners, seeing what was happening, ordered a three-month ban on all further land development while it drew up a greenbelt zoning law. By the time the "cooling off" period ended on November 10, the Board had set minimum lot sizes and made it illegal to fill in land too low to develop or to place any building closer than fifty feet from the edge of a body of water.

In late September of 1970, Governor Milliken stepped into the fray. In a letter to the Natural Resources Commission he acknowledged that the Commission's supervisor of wells was obliged to release oil and gas drilling permits upon request if all regulations were met, but he nevertheless asked that no further permits be issued "until you have completed the total reappraisal of leasing and drilling regulations."

19

"We just can't afford to take chances with our environment," he continued. "This is another instance of having to give as much consideration to ecology as technology." Referring to the Pigeon River Country, he said, "This is a unique area because it is in the heart of the limited elk range of Michigan. There appears to be unanswered questions regarding the impact of oil and gas drilling upon the aesthetic and environmental assets of the area."

DNR director Ralph MacMullan sensed a storm brewing. "We may well be on the verge of setting another far-sweeping precedent," he said. "It's a good bet oil people from across the nation will jump in here with both feet when threatened with the first victory of aesthetics over oil needs."

Members of the Natural Resources Commission agreed and ordered the supervisor of wells to stop issuing oil and gas drilling permits for sites in both the Pigeon River Country and the equally environmentally sensitive Jordan River Valley of Antrim County until further notice.

The oilmen were furious. Their representative Ray Markel told the commissioners, "You're going to have a lot of legal difficulties if you follow this suspension. We are private oilmen and are not going to sit still on this. We're going to fight it from the very first drop." G. R. Denison added that the Commission would face possible court action if it reneged on the lease contracts.

During the next few months public hearings were held all over Michigan to gather information and give everyone a chance to be heard. Ford Kellum and his allies showed up at every one of the hearings and continued protesting all drilling in the Pigeon River Country.

Gerald Eddy balked at all the pressure and officially established eighty-acre spacing restrictions for future drilling in Otsego and Kalkaska counties. "If conservation groups don't like the way the DNR is handling oil drilling matters in northern Michigan," he said, "they can try to get their lawmakers to change the laws."

Somewhat surprisingly, a voice of moderation came from the ranks of the oilmen. Jack Duran, a spokesman for Shell Oil, suggested that spacing restrictions be raised to permit only one well per 160 acres in order to prevent the drilling of unnecessary wells. Other oil firms took issue with Duran's proposal, however, denouncing it as no more than a move to appease conservationists. Official spacing restrictions remained at the eighty-acre level.

MacMullan made an unusually candid statement that August to the effect that he'd like to see the DNR sued to force it to authorize drilling in the Pigeon River Country, since under existing law it had no right to keep the oil companies from drilling a well on every eighty-acre tract of land that they had leased from the state. "I'd give anything if we'd had the foresight to see these things and had not leased the land," he said.

Prodded by the governor's office, members of the Natural Resources Commission drafted a new oil and gas leasing policy in December of 1970. It proved to be considerably more restrictive than the policy it replaced, prohibiting drilling within a quarter of a mile of any lake or principal stream to which the state held mineral rights, regardless of whether it was on state or public lands. An exception was granted for cases in which oil or gas under adjacent property could be drained away by a working well.

The Commission also banned drilling in all state parks and recreation areas, state forest campgrounds, and dedicated game areas, and it prohibited the development of a drilling area until the company holding the lease had received written approval from the area forester for locating access roads and disposing of destroyed forest products.

The Commission's new policy also stated that if a lease holder failed to begin development within three years, the lease would be terminated, although the company could apply for an extension through the DNR director if new problems had arisen in the area.

An editorial in the September 1970 issue of *Michigan Out-of-Doors*, the official publication of Michigan United Conservation Clubs, stated that the "discovery of oil and gas in the northern part of the Lower Peninsula within the past year has been termed 'a real tragedy.' MUCC thinks the term is correct. The tragedy began in Lansing in the DNR. It was the DNR which authorized drilling by the oil industry. The people of Michigan had a right to expect DNR to safeguard their best interests in the northern recreational areas. DNR didn't."

5
KELLUM QUITS DNR

Early in 1971, Michigan Consolidated Gas Company obtained authorization to build nearly fifty miles of natural gas transmission pipeline and related facilities in Otsego, Kalkaska, and Grand Traverse counties. The company entered into an agreement with Shell Oil to purchase natural gas from the Pigeon River Country, while Shell announced plans to build gas processing plants in Otsego and Kalkaska counties. The petroleum industry estimated that there were 98.5 billion cubic feet of gas reserves under Pigeon River Country.

At the beginning of 1971 the Michigan DNR was collecting about $41,000 a year from Shell Oil in royalties from the Charlton #1-4 well on Lost Cabin Trail, at an average of three dollars per barrel. It was estimated that the royalties could rise to $195,000 per year if the DNR were willing to permit Shell to pump more oil at the site.

Gerald Eddy announced that he planned to retire from his post as state supervisor of wells in late February. He had been chief of Michigan's Geological Survey Division before becoming DNR director in 1951. He held that position for thirteen years, resigning in 1964 to make way for Ralph MacMullan and return to his former post. As he was preparing to leave, Eddy said of the new rules the Natural Resources Commission had adopted that "They fill some important gaps that appeared in the old regulations."

On March 31, MacMullan finally responded to Ford Kellum's invitation to leave Lansing and have a look around the north country. Having done so, the DNR director had to admit that he was "appalled at the rate of development" that had followed on the heels of the intense publicity surrounding the Pigeon River Country and surrounding areas. He was particularly disturbed by what he saw at the Lake of the North and Wilderness Valley developments.

Nevertheless, in April Lansing DNR officials ignored the recommendations of field men and granted permission to Michigan Consolidated Gas Company to clear up to fifty feet alongside the Tin Shanty Bridge Trail for a pipeline route. The fifty feet later became eighty feet. Lansing also announced plans to allow a two-mile cut through the Black River Swamp for a pipeline. Field men had recommended that the ten-inch pipeline be laid down along existing roads, where a swath no more than thirty feet wide would have to be cut. Their request was completely ignored in Roscommon and Lansing, however, and permission was granted to cut a fifty-foot-wide path straight through elk and deer management areas and across the Black River.

That same month, Michigan attorney general Frank Kelley handed down a legal opinion stating that the DNR did in fact have the authority to deny oil drilling permits on already leased lands if drilling would threaten the environment. The opinion went even further, stating that the DNR was legally required to prevent drilling where it would cause "unnecessary damage to, or destruction of, the surface, soils, animal, fish or aquatic life" of the area or where it would "molest, spoil or destroy state-owned land." The opinion was based on laws that had been in force in Michigan since 1921.

On June 1, Kellum and other field men met with DNR personnel from Lansing and regional offices to draw up a list of areas in which oil drilling should be prohibited. The field men were unanimous in recommending that all of the Pigeon River Country should be placed off-limits to any further drilling. The Lansing officials were not at all happy with the opinions of the Gaylord men.

Ten days later the Natural Resources Commission ended its moratorium on issuing permits for drilling in northern Michigan. Attorney General Kelley said the NRC lacked "legal authority to withhold permits for leased lands on a blanket basis."

In mid-June Kellum reported that it had taken him five times as many hours of travel during the winter and spring of 1970-71 to find an elk in elk country than it had just three years earlier, and twice as many as it had the year before. The elk

The public is banned from some areas because of oil production, while roads rip through formerly wild terrain.

survey he conducted in 1971 yielded 147 sightings. "Man is driving elk out with oil exploration, loss of range, snowmobiles (running on oil survey lines) and other pressures caused by human activities," he concluded.

A *Detroit Free Press* editorial stated that Ralph MacMullan had spoken "with all the anger of a prophet" when he said that "We've goofed up every damn thing we've touched. Man has goofed up through his inordinant selfishness, which is just a new expression of the old animal instinct in us." By then the *Free Press* was supporting Kellum and his vision for the Pigeon River Country. The *Detroit News*, on the other hand, generally supported the oil and gas industry.

In response to an avalanche of recommendations, Michigan United Conservation Clubs, still leaderless after the death of James Rouman, honored Kellum with their Conservationist of the Year award at their convention in Escanaba in June. Governor Milliken presented the award, citing Kellum for his work in getting the DNR to formulate a new and better policy for the regulation of the state's oil and gas industry.

Prestigious as the MUCC honor was, Kellum had been even more impressed when the Michigan Audubon Society at Traverse City had awarded him its highest honor shortly before in recognition of his work with the Pigeon River Audubon Club and his "unselfish dedication to the true cause of conservation."

On July 21, 1971, Kellum unveiled a plan for establishing a 120-square-mile elk wilderness area in the heart of the Pigeon River Country, north and east of Gaylord. He pointed out that the DNR had authority to set aside the twenty-mile-long, six-mile-wide tract for special management to preserve its "scenic qualities" and its "unique natural habitat" for big game. The area in question consisted of about ninety percent state-owned lands and included the Pigeon River Research Station, which he suggested should be made the headquarters for the special area. Only 16.75 square miles of the proposed area was privately owned, and that land could be purchased as it became available in the future.

Kellum urged that road improvements, pipelines, power lines, oil and gas wells, development of recreational facilities, and off-road vehicles be prohibited in the proposed area. To protect its wild characteristics, he said, it might even be necessary to limit access to the area to hunters, fishermen, and other users if it looked at though they were threatening wildlife habitats there.

In August of 1968 a DNR wildlife survey of a 6,913-mile grid route in Pigeon River Country had turned up 110 elk calves. In 1969, the number had dropped to forty-eight. In 1970 it had been down to six. In 1971, survey crews searching for 709 hours had been able to find no more than three calves. Dick Moran, a wildlife researcher, concluded that the elk could "no longer survive in the thousands of acres" of Pigeon River Country because of the increasing human pressure in the area. Increased use of snowmobiles, camping, and other human activities were simply driving the elk out.

*   *   *

In May of 1970, Ford Kellum had stated that if the Charlton #1-4 well turned out to be a producer he would retire from the DNR and fight for the survival of his beloved Pigeon River Country from the outside. On August 19, 1971, he did just that.

More than two hundred people attended his retirement party at Gaylord. State wildlife chief Merrill "Pete" Petoskey served as emcee.

Noting the occasion, the *Otsego County Herald-Times* declared in an editorial that "Ford Kellum calls himself an 'uneducated professional.' He's only half right. A professional, he is. Uneducated, he is not. We would never play down the importance of a college degree but in the case of Ford Kellum's career, it wouldn't have improved anything. There is no room for improvement. He did an excellent job.

"It is a deep sense and desire to protect our environment that carried Ford down the wilderness path. There are few people around like Ford Kellum. No matter what the odds, he isn't one to give up without a fight. He has stood face-to-face with powerful oil companies and even high officials of the DNR, all for the cause of protecting valuable state lands, water and wildlife from destruction. He's not ready to give up yet. His plan to save part of the Pigeon River Country proves his lasting devotion to the cause of environmental protection."

Early in September Kellum met with fellow members of the Audubon Society Jerry Myers and Dave Smethurst to discuss the formation of a Pigeon River Country Association to help fight the battles they knew lay before them. Smethurst became the first president of the PRCA.

Now completely free to speak out on all of the issues, Kellum went on the road, crisscrossing Michigan to speak to every group he could find. He illustrated many of his talks with color slides he had taken during his years of service in the Pigeon River Country area. They gave a clear and impressive indication of just what would be lost if oil and gas exploration and drilling were permitted to continue.

Many of the groups Kellum addressed wanted to see the area in person, and so he volunteered to serve as their guide. Among the groups that made the tour were members of the influential Michigan Audubon Society and the Michigan State Federation of Women's Clubs.

6
PIGEON RIVER
COUNTRY ASSOCIATION

As 1972 began, the Michigan Bear Hunters Association presented Kellum with its highest honor, the Sparky Hale Award. Long one of the strongest conservation organizations in Michigan, the MBHA was founded by Carl T. Johnson, who went on to become a member of the Natural Resources Commission and a strong supporter of Kellum's objectives.

The MBHA cited Kellum for "many times laying his job on the line to protect Michigan's natural resources." It was also noted that he had been repeatedly passed over for promotions within the DNR because he had refused to be muzzled by his superiors. Even so, the Association's citation noted, his persistence had in the end led to the formulation of a new state oil policy.

The newly formed Pigeon River Country Association met to revise the boundaries of the proposed Pigeon River Country tract. Kellum had originally proposed an area of 120 square miles made up of ninety percent state-owned lands. The new proposal was for a 125-square-mile tract made up of ninety-six percent state-owned lands and a substantial buffer zone of state holdings, all of which should be kept free from development. Kellum estimated that there were six hundred elk, one hundred black bears, and one hundred bobcats living in the proposed area at that time.

The PRCA gained approval for the plan from every governmental and conservation group in Otsego and Cheboygan counties and most of the state's Audubon Clubs, the Michigan Bear

Black bear   Bobcat PHOTO COURTESY OF MICHIGAN D.N.R.

Hunters Association, Michigan United Conservation Clubs, the Sierra Club, Trout Unlimited, Michigan Bowhunters Association, the Wilderness Society, and the Women's Federation of Northern Michigan. In February Kellum was elected to the board of directors of the Michigan Audubon Society, which gave him yet more clout in his efforts. But the PRCA still noted that it was running into resistance from the DNR's Lansing office.

The DNR wasn't the only problem. Opposition to the PRCA plan was immediately forthcoming from all of the major oil companies, Michigan Consolidated Gas, Consumers Power Company, and some private individuals who owned land in and around the Pigeon River Country.

Later that January, Ralph MacMullan vetoed oil company requests to open up the Black River Swamp west of Lost Cabin Trail to oil drilling under a unitization plan that would require that all drilling be done by a single company rather than by a number of individual firms. DNR field men recommended that if drilling was going to be allowed at all, it should be done from

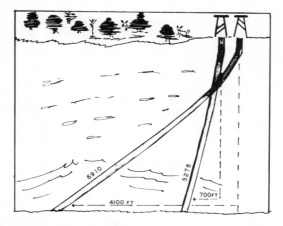

"Slant hole" drilling enables the oil companies to reach petroleum deposits as much as 4,100 feet away from the drilling site. Some California drillers have tapped deposits as much as 4,800 feet away from the well, but only at depths of 3,000 feet.

centrally located platforms by means of slant drilling rather by clusters of wells scattered throughout the area. The oil companies complained that slant drilling would be "unreasonably expensive" and probably wouldn't work in any case.

Among those within the Natural Resources Commission who pressed hardest for the slant-drilling proposal was Carl Johnson. At his own expense, Johnson made a western tour to investigate the feasibility of the process. He came back convinced that it could in fact work in the Pigeon River Country and wherever else the potential of environmental damage was a concern.

Kellum remained firm in his conviction that no sort of drilling would be safe in Pigeon River Country, however. "We don't want any kind of wells in there," he insisted. "It would mean more people, more trucks, more noise, and more chance for accidents." He urged that the Charlton #1-4 well be capped and saved "for the day when we might have an emergency."

Shell Oil Company vigorously opposed such a move and pressed on for another permit to drill one mile south of the Charlton #1- 4 site. DNR officials were expected to approve the request on the grounds that roads and pipelines were already in place for the producing well and a second well would not appreciably increase the chance for environmental damage in the area. PRCA members objected strongly, charging that approval would set the stage for a domino effect: well after well would be approved on the grounds that each added only a small amount of damage to an environment that had already been harmed by preceding wells, until in the end the whole area would be ruined by development.

Lansing DNR planners began working on a concept for setting up four "influence zones" in the Pigeon River Country based on the bodies of water, travel routes, forest wildlife, and special features they contained. Some DNR officials opposed designating all of Pigeon River Country as a wilderness area because they feared that protecting it completely in this way would only lead to the overdevelopment of surrounding areas. The proposed "influence zones" study was expected to take ten years.

Among the PRCA's strong supporters was Dr. Joseph L. Sax, the University of Michigan law professor who had written the Michigan Environmental Protection Act of 1970. In a letter to Glen Sheppard, publisher of *The North Woods Call*, Sax blasted the DNR's contention that it could "find no legal grounds for denying Amoco permission to drill" in the Pigeon River Country because the attorney general had said that "the DNR cannot deny drilling permits on the grounds that scenery will be damaged."

Sax noted that "the attorney general's opinion itself notes that the state's standard leases contain a very broad provision stating that the lease 'shall be subject to the rules and regulations of the DNR now or hereafter in force . . . all of which rules and regulations are made a part and condition of this lease.' Such a provision gives DNR very broad regulatory powers indeed. Moreover, the general statute broadly prohibits 'the unnecessary damage to or destruction of the surface, soils, animals, fish or aquatic life or property from or by oil and gas operations.'

"In addition to this, we now have the Environmental Protection Act of 1970 which itself prohibits all conduct that does, or is likely to, 'impair . . . natural resources and the public trust.'

"Finally, the case cited by the attorney general on aesthetic regulation, even if it were applicable in this situation, was decided in 1937 and the courts countrywide have been moving dramatically away from this restrictive view in recent years as concern for environmental values has increased. There is certainly plenty of legal basis for trying to control degradation of scenic values and it is inexcusable for our officials to hide behind narrowly restrictive interpretations of their powers.

"It may be that the meek will inherit the earth but the kind of earth they inherit may not be worth having," Sax concluded.

* * *

In May of 1972, William Turney, assistant chief of the DNR water quality control division, told the Natural Resources Commission that nobody knew the condition of Michigan's oil pipelines. For all they knew, miles of pipe might be rusty, weak, and defective, and Turney estimated that it would take as much as a year to compile an accurate assessment. He also said that the DNR was so tied up investigating oil leaks and spills that it didn't have the time or resources to compile such information.

Adding to Turney's comments, Arthur Slaughter, Gerald Eddy's successor as DNR geology chief, noted that the number of older producing wells in the state was increasing. In fact, forty percent of the oil being produced in Michigan was coming from older, "marginal" wells that were already past their prime. This was an ominous figure, because marginal wells constitute a greater risk to the environment. As profit from a well declines, so does an operator's incentive to do a good job of maintaining the related pipelines and storage facilities.

Turney reported that there had been 266 reported oil spills in 1970, 166 of which posed a threat to watercourses. In 1971 there had been 325 spills reported, with sixty percent endangering waterways. In 1972 there had already been ninety reports by May, forty-nine near water. One faulty oil pipeline near Lake St. Helen had leaked into the south branch of the Au Sable River for several weeks before it was detected that spring. Little harm was done to the river's fish population, said Turney, but the damage to adjoining wildlife habitats was substantial.

During the same meeting, the commissioners approved lease sales on nearly 500,000 additional acres of state lands in northern Michigan from which they anticipated receiving revenues of between three and six million dollars from the oil companies. The Commission expected to place about 145,000 acres of the new block being leased into "nondevelopment" status, which would mean that oil companies would not be allowed to drill on the lands themselves, although they would still be allowed to drain off oil beneath the areas through wells sunk on adjoining lands.

The new lease sales were approved quickly to ensure that revenues would reach the Michigan treasury before the fiscal year began on July 1. DNR lands chief Robert G. Wood later revealed that the director of the Bureau of Progams and Budget, John T. Dempsey, had put pressure on the DNR to speed up sales of more oil leases in addition to suggesting that some lands be reclassified to permit development in order to generate more money for the state.

DNR deputy director Charles Harris warned against such action, however. "We're skating on pretty thin ice if we start changing nondevelopment lands to development status," he said, predicting that they'd be sued by the Sierra Club and other conservation groups if they made such a move.

Meanwhile, the DNR's Oil Advisory Board, made up entirely of members of the oil and gas industry, scoffed at the idea that the Pigeon River Country had any real appeal for the people of Michigan and refused to accept any testimony from groups requesting that the area be dedicated as a permanent wilderness area under a zoned plan.

"If DNR goes along with the Oil Advisory Board, we can kiss the Pigeon River Country goodbye," said Ford Kellum. "The only thing that can save it now is a widespread uprising by the little people of Michigan to let the governor, their legislators, and the DNR know they think the area is worth saving. This land is priceless, and it belongs to all of us right now. Are we going to just let them turn it over to private interests?"

7
A NEW SLANT ON
DRILLING

Later in May of 1972, personnel from the DNR's information and education section made a tour of the Pigeon River Country, with people from Shell Oil Company serving as guides, as part of a training mission. DNR people had invited Ford Kellum too, but he was later "uninvited"—at the request of Shell Oil, he maintained.

"I didn't really care, but I feel it was a sort of cheap thing to do," he said. All DNR officials in Lansing denied that it had ever happened, but Kellum knew for a fact that "the same DNR executive who invited me, then uninvited me." He decided to shrug it off. "I was busy at the time anyway," he summed up.

In June, Harry Whiteley, then chairman of the Natural Resources Commission, visited the Pigeon River Country along with Charles Gunther, executive assistant to Ralph MacMullan. They were guided by Dave Smethurst, president of the Pigeon River Country Association. "We don't want this land designated a 'wilderness area' where no one is allowed," Smethurst told them. "We think it should be established as a special resource management area so that it can be used most wisely."

Whiteley said he feared they'd wind up with "a north woods ghetto" if they didn't have proper control on land use in northern Michigan, and he said that it was the Commission's job to see that that didn't happen. "First we had the moratorium and now we've ordered that every application for a drilling permit be brought up before the DNR director and possibly the entire commission before it's granted. I really don't think we can shut down the oil industry, but we sure can make it responsible for its impact on the environment," Whiteley insisted. "Personally, I don't care if we never have another oil well in this area."

"Our attorneys are poised and ready to go," Smethurst told them. "The first well drilling permit granted on state lands north of the Charlton #1-4 discovery well will result in a suit being filed." He indicated that the legal action might be taken up under the new Michigan Environmental Protection Act.

A test of the Commission's new determination came later in June. McClure Oil Company (Michigan Oil) of Alma acquired lease rights to lands on the Round Lake Trail just two miles east of the Pigeon River Research Station. The former lease owner had been refused a drilling permit and sold the lease to McClure Oil, which hoped to force a test case in their favor with some help from political friends in Lansing.

The Lansing DNR unofficially let it be known that it would reject the McClure application for the same reason it had turned down the application of the previous lease owner: it would involve opening up a wild area.

McClure charged that snowmobilers, off-road vehicles, campers, and other human incursions were more detrimental to the area than an oil well would be. The company noted that an operating oil well generates only 50 decibels of noise, compared to 86 decibels for a logging truck, 90 for a motorcycle, 104 for a snowmobile, and 115 for a chainsaw. DNR personnel countered by pointing out that well operations go on twenty-four hours a day, whereas the other sorts of noise are only intermittent, and so give the wildlife some relief.

Smethurst stated that the PRCA would seek a partial curb on all people pressures and noise in the Pigeon River Country in addition to doing everything possible to keep the additional menace of oil drilling out of the area.

As representatives of the PRCA, Smethurst and Kellum both regularly attended meetings of the Natural Resources Commission. At a July 10 Commission meeting in Cadillac, the two gained a sympathetic ear from DNR assistant director Gene Gazlay, who recommended that the Commission designate the Pigeon River Country as a special resource management area. The recommendation was approved, but nothing was said about an oil drilling policy for the tract.

Meanwhile, the lease rights on 490,000 acres of state land in northern Michigan were auctioned off. Drillers paid a record $9.2 million—twice what the DNR had predicted, and more than eight times the previous record for a state auction of mineral rights ($1.1 million in 1968). Shell Oil turned in the high bid of $1,000 an acre for 160 acres in Otsego County, three miles south of Johannesburg.

The PRCA, still composed of only forty members from a five-county area, was meeting regularly with members of the Natural Resources Commission and the Michigan Oil and Gas Association to see if some common ground could be found.

John T. McDonald, manager of gas, land, and right-of-way for Northern Michigan Exploration Company (Consumers Power) said that only 675 of the 1.5 million acres of north country would be needed for producing well sites. He failed to mention all the additional acreage that would be needed for the access roads, pipelines, power lines, and other developments that would have to be brought in to get the oil and gas from those well sites to where it could be used.

In August the north's first slant-drilled well was unveiled by Shell Oil at the Charlton #1-4 site. It was designed to tap a pool of oil nearly a mile away, on the far side of the Black River Swamp. If it was successful, the company was prepared to drill another slant well to a second off-site source.

Earlier the oil companies had complained that slant well drilling would be impossible—and indeed, it was more expensive than traditional drilling—but since the DNR had refused to grant Shell drilling permits in locations they had deemed too fragile, the oilmen found that the new technology was not so impossible after all.

Meanwhile, McClure Oil was being persistent in its way, too. The rumor was that McClure was ready to fight the DNR's denial of a drilling permit for the Round Lake Trail site all the way to the U.S. Supreme Court if necessary. On September 13 the DNR named Frederic S. Abood as chief hearing officer to preside over the appeal case in the McClure matter. The lands in question had originally been leased in October of 1968.

8
GAZLAY REPLACES MacMULLAN

Dr. Ralph A. MacMullan, director of the DNR, died suddenly of a heart attack on September 23, 1972, at the age of 55.

Beginning with the old Department of Conservation in 1946 as a wildlife biologist, he had worked his way up the ladder to become assistant chief of the game division in 1962. He replaced Gerald Eddy as director on May 1, 1964, and announced that he would make efforts to improve the direction of what was to be called the *new* Department of Natural Resources.

A month after MacMullan's death, Gene Gazlay became the new DNR director at age 48. Like MacMullan, he had joined the department in 1948 as a wildlife biologist and had since risen in its ranks. He had been MacMullan's assistant director since 1968 and had served as acting director in the period between his former boss's death and his official promotion.

One of Gazlay's first concerns was the need to end what he referred to as "the growing problem of rural slums in the northern part of the state." He announced that "My goals and my objectives will be very similar to those Mac pursued with so much drive and energy and, certainly, success in the past few years."

DNR foresters and biologists were put to work on a preliminary plan to manage a 120-square-mile tract of the Pigeon River Country as a special area, but not as a wilderness area. The decision had already been made to bar snowmobiles and off-road vehicles from some sections of the area. It had also been decided that trail roads in some parts of the forest would be closed to all traffic in order to create more quiet spots for elk and other wildlife. To further improve deer and elk habitats, oil well sites were to be approved only along the outer fringes of the area, commercial harvesting of timber would be allowed only under close supervision, and controls on camping and canoeing in the area would be tightened.

Gazlay agreed with the foresters and biologists who felt that it would be too drastic a measure to designate the lands as a wilderness area, since that would rule out virtually all activity in the area—including habitat management. He believed that proposals to limit and control recreational uses of the area would also serve to keep drillers out.

A direct example of how the DNR's new regulations could help to protect the lands came up in November of 1972. It was then that Jim Welch, an alert young reporter for the *Otsego County Herald-Times*, learned of plans to run a high-speed road rally right through the heart of the Pigeon River Country. The two-thousand-mile-long "Press On Regardless" rally was set to begin in Detroit and roar through the Pigeon River during what happened to be the elk mating season.

Race officials and sponsors had not applied to the DNR for any of the necessary permits to run a course through the area's narrow trails. Running high-speed vehicles through the area's twisting roadways and soft sands between 2:00 and 4:00 a.m. would clearly have been out of line with the department's new guidelines. When Welch exposed the race plan in his paper, officials quickly agreed to chart a new course that would bypass Pigeon River Country.

* * *

As 1973 began, Governor Milliken gave the order to make the DNR the one regulatory agency for all of the state's environmental matters as well natural resource matters. The new centralization of controls was set to take effect on March 15. Milliken said that it would bring responsibility for all land, water, and air resources under the DNR and "make the buck stop there."

Gazlay candidly told the members of the Natural Resources Commission that the DNR's handling of the Pigeon River Country case would probably establish a precedent. "If the oil industry can force the DNR to issue drilling permits in areas which will be ruined by oil activity," he warned, "the people of Michigan stand to lose the best outdoor areas of Michigan."

DNR lands chief Robert Wood told the commissioners that on the average the state was earning about one dollar per acre from leases held by the oil industry on 1,450,000 acres of state-owned lands. Of this, $101,118 was coming from the Charlton #1-4 well in the Pigeon River Country.

In February, freshman state legislator Mark Thompson of Rogers City bluntly told amazed newsmen that "I don't want anybody from the DNR talking to any of my constituents." He expressed strong opposition to a temporary DNR policy designed to bring oil drillers on private lands under the same set of strict environmental controls as those that applied to drilling on state-owned lands. The same objections were voiced by state senator Gary Byker of Holland as well as representatives of Shell Oil, Amoco, and several other oil firms.

The uproar rose in response to temporary rules that had been adopted by the DNR in January and that were set to come up for consideration by the Natural Resources Commission in March. The DNR had drafted the new policy after an oil well had been drilled right on the banks of a creek in Kalkaska County, threatening a damaging oil spill there.

Continued publicity about the Pigeon River Country was serving to attract more people to the area. Poachers were among those entering the area in greatly increased numbers, and the relatively small herd of wild elk there was being seriously threatened. *The North Woods Call* set up a special "Poacher Patrol" reward system to pay for information on violators while protecting the anonymity of the informants. The project ultimately became too expensive for the little Charlevoix-based newspaper and was taken over by the Lansing office of Michigan United Conservation Clubs.

The Natural Resources Commission decided to hold its May 1973 meeting in Gaylord, mostly at the insistence of Ford Kellum, who protested in a letter to Governor Milliken that the "little people" were not being heard. Kellum's objection stemmed mostly from an extended hearing to gather information on the Pigeon River Country that Frederic Abood was conducting for the DNR in Lansing.

Kellum attended a portion of the twenty-day hearing and was able to present some testimony, but he acknowledged that he and the lawyer for the Pigeon River Country Association were "pretty much overshadowed by a whole flock of high-powered lawyers hired by all the oil companies that want to drill in our last remaining wilderness." As it turned out, most of the four

Drilling went on in the Pigeon River Country winter and summer.

thousand pages of testimony that was given during the Abood hearing was indeed given by oil company representatives.

During the course of their Gaylord meeting, the members of the Natural Resources Commission heard widespread opposition to further drilling in northern Michigan. Northern Exploration Company, Shell, and Amoco proposed combining their leases (together they held ninety percent of the leases that had been granted in the Pigeon River Country) into three or four broad management units in order to limit the number of drilling sites, pipelines, roads, and other development that would be necessary in the area.

Ray Pfeiffer of the DNR's forestry division also presented his long-awaited proposal for the Pigeon River Country at the

Gaylord meeting. Work on the plan had begun with a survey by Lee Eckstrom, who had been replaced by Pfeiffer in January. The proposal turned out to be "surprisingly close" to what the members of the Pigeon River Country Association had been seeking. Among the changes proposed by the plan was an expansion of the protected area from 125 square miles to 140 square miles. The oil industry maintained that the plan would not be workable.

Another topic came up for discussion at the Gaylord meeting that was only incidentally related to the Pigeon River Country issue: the matter of gas eruptions and blowholes at Williamsburg. The area northeast of Traverse City had experienced a series of ground collapses that began on April 15, 1973, and continued to endanger the small community's population. Dozens of people had had to be evacuated to escape the hazards of gas inhalation and explosions.

Arthur Slaughter, the DNR's supervisor of wells, came close to blaming Amoco for the fiasco at Williamsburg, but he stopped short of doing so. In the end the situation led to the adoption of new safeguards for drilling all oil and gas wells in Michigan.

In connection with the Gaylord meeting, some of the commissioners who had not yet seen the Pigeon River Country firsthand were taken on a tour. Kellum was not invited to go along with the party, and, fearing a possible whitewash, he led his own tour of several carloads of newsmen on a more extended tour of the area than the commissioners were receiving.

The issue of dangers associated with oil exploration came to light again in May, when children brought Kellum an explosive charge that they had found in a hole. The hole and the charge were placed as part of the oil exploration process: reflected shock waves from underground explosion gave geologists some idea of where they could find the richest deposits in the Niagaran Reef formation far below. The Geophysical Oil Company had drilled the hole, one among many, and left the charge in place over the long Memorial Day weekend for detonation later. Similar explosive charges were subsequently found near the Grass Lake Campground close to the Pigeon River Country headquarters.

9

THE ABOOD RECOMMENDATIONS

Although small in membership, the Pigeon River Country Association was named Michigan's "Conservation Organization of the Year" by Michigan United Conservation Clubs at their convention in June of 1973. While not agreeing with all MUCC views, the PRCA had decided to join the coalition of more than four hundred state clubs in order to give its voice a wider sounding board throughout Michigan.

The following month, Paul Leach, the man who some time earlier had been selected to replace the late James L. Rouman as MUCC executive director, resigned from that post. It was generally understood that Leach was the unfortunate victim of a power struggle that had been going on within MUCC ranks since the time when Rouman was still chief.

Addressing the Natural Resources Commission at a Petoskey meeting in August, Pat Huber, a geological engineer for Shell Oil, presented another plan for pooling oil company resources to remove oil and gas from the Pigeon River Country with slant well drilling. Shell had already sunk one such directional well from the Charlton #1-4 site, and if the technique were used more extensively, Huber argued, the oil companies could tap more underground oil pools with fewer overall drilling sites, roads, and pipelines, and with less risk to the area's watercourses. He also indicated a willingness to lay longer pipelines along existing roads rather than using shorter direct lines through the swamps to pump the oil away from the sites.

Huber's proposal amounted to one of the first public admissions by a member of the oil industry that slant drilling was feasible in northern Michigan. Both Ford Kellum and Natural Resources Commission member Carl T. Johnson, long familiar with the Pigeon River Country as a hunter, had maintained since 1970 that the technique would work in Michigan's more fragile areas, but the oil industry had steadfastly denied it.

While he had the commissioners' attention, Huber gave them a short course in the area's geology. He explained that the oil and gas deposits under the Pigeon River Country were located in thick beds of salt and ranged from eighty to five hundred acres in size. Most oilmen were convinced that the richest deposits were located in the southern portion of the Pigeon River Country in Otsego County and that they diminished as they ran north into Cheboygan County.

Since the best estimate was that there were ten to thirty oil and gas deposits worth tapping in each of the prime townships, it was assumed that about twenty central drilling sites per thirty-six-square-mile township should be enough to enable the oil companies to access the underground riches. Each central drilling site, which would support multiple slant wells, would take up about five and a half acres—so no more than about 106 acres of each township would be required for the well sites themselves. Allowing another eleven acres for roads and forty acres for collection and processing facilities, the total space required per township would be only 157 acres out of 23,000 (with an additional 95 acres required for cross-county pipelines throughout the whole system on top of that). Huber went on to estimate that all of the oil could be removed from the elk country within twenty-five years and that the oil companies could thus be out of the area completely by the year 2000.

If Huber had expected some sort of rubber stamp approval of his proposal, he was in for a disappointment. Gazlay backed Johnson and other commissioners in turning thumbs down on the plan. Even so, Gazlay's caution was not yet representative of the DNR as a whole. In a September 1 UPI wire story, Governor Milliken berated the DNR for its "arrogant, callous, high-handed and bureaucratic" methods of dealing with the public. He called for a "more sensitive and responsive" approach.

Gazlay appreciated the validity of the governor's complaints. "I can't do anything but agree with him," he said. "One thing that certainly is going to be important is indoctrinating our people. This is one of those things you have to do every once in a while anyway. We're going to have to make sure with our people that the left hand knows what the right hand is doing. It's not something that's all that simple, or obviously we could have done something about it by now."

On September 12, Hilary Snell of the Natural Resources Commission cited a potential threat to DNR regulations. Wolverine Oil of Grand Rapids had requested a permit to drill a well on private land nine miles northeast of Atlanta in Montmorency County. The proposed site was on a small knoll surrounded by a marsh that drained into the Black River near the edge of the Pigeon River Country. The project would involve filling in part of the swamp and building an access road, culverts, and a crossing over Rattlesnake Creek.

DNR field men were solidly opposed to granting the permit. Their opinion was seconded by Snell, who argued that it would set a precedent for permitting drilling on the banks of rivers and lakes, and by Carl Johnson, who noted that the Rattlesnake Hill area was one of the few good bobcat habitats left in northern Michigan.

Johnson asked why the deposit couldn't be tapped by directional drilling from a site half a mile to the east that was located on an already existing road and was distant from any watercourse. Oilmen complained that it would cost an additional $100,000 to sink a slant well from that site, although a spokesman for Shell Oil said that his company wouldn't rule out the possibility of a slant well there. No immediate decision was made.

On October 10-11 the Natural Resources Commission met to consider the application of Michigan Oil Company for a permit to drill a well at the Round Lake Trail Campground in the Pigeon River Country. It was at this meeting that Frederic Abood presented his long-awaited recommendation, based on the four thousand pages of testimony (most of it given by representatives of the oil industry) he had received during the twenty-day hearing he had held earlier that year.

In essence, Abood recommended that permits be issued to the oil industry to drill in all parts of the Pigeon River Country, and he stressed that in his opinion the DNR had no choice but to approve the permit to drill at the Round Lake (Corwith #1-22) site.

Abood stated that as long as the 145-square-mile Pigeon River Country area was already being used for twenty-three other types of activities—hunting, camping, trail biking, fishing, and other recreational "disturbances"—he felt that drilling would

Round Lake Campground and the charming trail leading to it typify the beauty to be found in the Pigeon River Country.

not do any more harm to the area. He acknowledged that some of the testimony received from expert witnesses during the course of his hearing had revealed that the fragile habitats of elk, bears, bobcats, and other sensitive wildlife would be "seriously damaged" by all of the ongoing activities, but he maintained that oil and gas drilling would constitute little additional harm.

Just prior to Abood's presentation, DNR deputy director Charles Harris had presented an impressive forty-four-page booklet outlining the department's management plans for the Pigeon River Country. The plan called for designating roughly one third of the entire tract—including the Corwith area—as elk range. It also recommended adopting special management techniques to protect bears, bobcats, and eagles, all of which were endangered species within the Pigeon River Country.

Bald Eagle
PHOTO COURTESY OF MICHIGAN D.N.R.

"Truck traffic, clanking and hammering of construction or repair, engine and motor noises and fast-moving vehicles are all very disruptive, especially if continuous," the report stated. To protect the area from noise that would harm wildlife habitats, the plan called for closing many of the open trails and limiting some sections to walk-in activities. (Some of these proposals closely reflected the ideas of P. S. Lovejoy, who was the first to seek to preserve his beloved "Big Wild.") The plan did propose permitting snowmobiling, trail biking, and similar forms of recreation, however, in areas where the noise would constitute less of a disturbance.

"There's a lot of difference between transitory noise, caused by recreation, and that caused by a permanent installation like an oil and gas operation," noted Pigeon River Country Association president Dave Smethurst. "If the commission goes along with Abood's suggestions, it will be the end of the Pigeon River Country," he continued. "Not only that, but it will encourage the oil industry to challenge the DNR on every other piece of state land where they now hold leases but haven't been allowed to drill up to now."

In November public hearings were held in Lansing and Gaylord to consider a forty-seven-page recommendation that had been commissioned from the Interstate Oil Compact Commission by the DNR at a cost of $5,000. Its audacity left a lot of mouths hanging open in shock.

Entitled "An Evaluation of Oil and Gas Regulatory Control in Michigan," the document recommended that the Natural Resources Commission be barred from observing field geology sites that threatened damage to the environment and from interfering in other ways in matters involving oil and gas drilling. The report also proposed that the geology division be separated from the DNR and given full authority over all oil policies.

If adopted, said Kellum, the IOCC's proposals would in effect negate all of the state's environmental protection laws and "eliminate all public participation in decisions on where wells should be drilled."

Speaking in December at the Michigan Environmental Awards program in Lake City, Kellum stated that "Our greatest threat to the environment is the energy conglomerate and the lack of proper land-use planning. Big energy, along with the energy people, have the money, legal talent, and political input to do just about as they see fit. It seems that it must fall back on the average citizen—how concerned he is, how he votes, and how he can organize his support with as many other concerned organizations—to get what is best for the most people for the longest period of time."

At the same meeting, Dave Smethurst reminded the audience that "only when by-passing bureaucracy did we make any progress with the Pigeon River Country." He also criticized the DNR for spending over a year on developing a management plan for the Pigeon River Country and then not taking any action to adopt it. "The DNR should get off dead-center," he said. "Public interest must replace self-interest. Values must change if we are even to survive."

E. M. "Matt" Laitala, chairman of the Natural Resources Commission, spoke up at that body's December 1973 meeting to deliver a broadside against environmentalists in general. He suggested that "too much emphasis is being placed on fun and frolic" in Michigan, and "not enough on oil, forest products, and other values." He went on to say that "Elk aren't all that important. People are our first concern." During previous meetings he had generally supported oil drilling and commercial forest harvesting on public lands and had dismissed the public's desire for recreational areas as "frivolous."

Laitala was the only commissioner to vote against adopting the proposed management plan for the Pigeon River Country. The five other commissioners at the meeting gave their full endorsement to the proposal that had been presented at the October meeting.

DNR director Gene Gazlay challenged Laitala's remarks, maintaining that adequate recreational resources were vital to Michigan's economy and to the mental health of its people. He argued that many of the state's social problems could be eased if its citizens had more access to "good, wholesome outdoor recreation." Social pressures were especially acute in the cities in the state's southern counties, said Gazlay, where it was difficult for the "people who need it most to find the proper types of recreation." As a trained biologist, he noted that "people penned up in a city with no escape can develop the same type of mental attitudes as wild animals confined to cages."

The new policy called for the DNR to "protect and maintain the natural beauty of [the state's] forests and waters, to sustain a healthy elk herd and wildlife populations and to practice management and wise use of all its resources."

The policy also specified that in areas where cutting would be permitted to aid wildlife, "to avoid disturbance during the critical time of nesting, young-bearing and the early weeks of life of wild young, off-road activities of logging will not be permitted from April 15 through June 30 in either elk range or wildlife habitat management areas."

In addition, the plan called for closing some roads and banning all motorized vehicles (including snowmobiles, trail bikes, and cars) from the area as well as returning some segments to their natural wild state.

As an aid to wildlife in the Pigeon River Country, motorized vehicles have been banned from some former trails, and food patches have been planted.

10

NORTH COUNTRY PRESSURES

As 1973 was ending, the north country oil boom was bringing thousands of new people into the area, putting heavy pressure on local governments. Schools were becoming grossly overcrowded. Royalties from oil and gas produced on state-owned lands were going into the Michigan treasury and not into local coffers.

One of the hardest hit areas was Kalkaska County, where residents repeatedly refused to vote for tax increases to finance the construction of new classrooms. At nearly every Natural Resources Commission meeting, commissioner Carl Johnson worked to get a higher oil tax so that some funds could be redirected to alleviate the problems of the oil-producing areas themselves. The Michigan legislature, heavily lobbied by oil interests, steadfastly ignored such a remedy.

The Pigeon River Country controversy was still raging in January of 1974, when DNR forestry chief Ted Daw announced that a 140-square-mile tract would officially be designated a state forest on the thirty-first of the month. He announced that Jerry Lawrence would be in charge of the area, assisted by forest technician Jerry Myers.

Meanwhile, Peter Vellenga, Gaylord attorney for the Pigeon River Country Association, charged Frederic Abood with having taken false testimony from oil company witnesses in the course of directing his hearing for the DNR. Vellenga pointed out that the oil company personnel who testified had no credentials as experts on wildlife or fishery management or any other environmental matters, and that their one-sided testimony could lead to the formation of policies that would result in serious damage to the Pigeon River Country.

Vellenga charged that Abood repeatedly ignored testimony from DNR biologists Dick Moran, Bob Strong, El Harger, and Nels Johnson that the Corwith #1-22 well sought by Michigan Oil Company would be highly damaging to several wildlife species. Not insignificantly, during a period of relatively rapid promotions within the DNR, not one of these four biologists was to receive any advancement for a number of years. Kellum later charged that it was the DNR's method of punishing them for having given testimony that they had been warned not to give.

Vellenga stated that he expected support from assistant state attorney general Jerry Maslowski in pressing his contention that Abood's decision was legally incorrect. The matter was crucial because if the Natural Resources Commission rejected Abood's decision, Michigan Oil was expected to appeal its action in the courts, and PRCA members were not sure that they could raise enough money for the court battles that would ensue. Prior to this time most of the PRCA's legal help had been donated.

By February it was beginning to look very much as though the DNR was getting ready to push for the sort of plan that Kellum had long been advocating for the Pigeon River Country. This impression was reinforced by the fact that Ned Caveney was appointed to be the first manager of the brand new Pigeon River Country State Forest, the boundaries of which had been redrawn to include portions of three other adjacent state forests in the area northeast of Gaylord in Otsego and Montmorency counties.

Caveney moved into the old Pigeon River Research Station in the middle of February to set up the area's new headquarters. Prior to that he had worked out of Traverse City, where he was credited with laying out the Sand Lakes Quiet Area in Grand Traverse and Kalkaska counties. In general, Caveney's career gave evidence of a practical concern for the environment, and Kellum applauded his appointment as guardian of the Pigeon River Country.

During the February meetings of the Natural Resources Commission in Lansing, Byron Gallagher, the attorney for Michigan Oil Company, tried to prevent commissioner Joan Wolfe from voting on Pigeon River Country matters by charging that doing so would involve her in a conflict of interest. It seemed that prior to her appointment to the Commission, Wolfe had

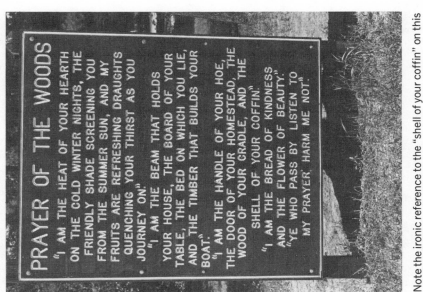

PRAYER OF THE WOODS

"I AM THE HEAT OF YOUR HEARTH ON THE COLD WINTER NIGHTS, THE FRIENDLY SHADE SCREENING YOU FROM THE SUMMER SUN, AND MY FRUITS ARE REFRESHING DRAUGHTS QUENCHING YOUR THIRST AS YOU JOURNEY ON."

"I AM THE BEAM THAT HOLDS YOUR HOUSE, THE BOARD OF YOUR TABLE, THE BED ON WHICH YOU LIE, AND THE TIMBER THAT BUILDS YOUR BOAT."

"I AM THE HANDLE OF YOUR HOE, THE DOOR OF YOUR HOMESTEAD, THE WOOD OF YOUR CRADLE, AND THE SHELL OF YOUR COFFIN"

"I AM THE BREAD OF KINDNESS AND THE FLOWER OF BEAUTY."

"YE WHO PASS BY LISTEN TO MY PRAYER HARM ME NOT."

Ford Kellum, left, with forester Ned Caveney.

Note the ironic reference to the "shell of your coffin" on this sign in the Pigeon River Country.

53

been a member of the West Michigan Environmental Action Council, which had just entered the Pigeon River Country case as a friend of the court in behalf of the DNR and was joining the PRCA in the legal battle over the controversial Corwith #1-22 oil well case. Wolfe was generally considered to be the swing vote on the seven-member Commission.

The West Michigan Environmental Action Council had gained entry to Michigan Oil's court case after claiming that Frederic Abood had overlooked several important aspects of the state and federal Environmental Protection Acts in recommending that the Corwith #1-22 well drilling permit be granted.

*　　*　　*

On February 24, 1974, just twenty-one months after the death of Ralph MacMullan, DNR director Gene Gazlay suffered a heart attack. Significantly incapacitated, Gazlay was able to provide only extremely limited service to the DNR until a second heart attack caused his death on June 30. In the interim, the Natural Resources Commission appointed Dave Jenkins to be acting director. Jenkins, a deputy director of the DNR with a background in wildlife biology, made it clear that he would not accept a permanent appointment to the tension-ridden post.

Toward spring, assistant attorney general Jerry Maslowski told the Natural Resources Commission that the proposed Corwith #1-22 oil well that Michigan Oil wanted to sink would be "an environmental insult. God help the resource if you allow it to be drilled!" Vellenga and Maslowski agreed that during the course of the Abood hearing McClure's attorneys had failed to refute testimony that the proposed well would threaten elk, bears, and other wildlife in the Pigeon River Country.

On April 12 the Commission formally denied a drilling permit for the Corwith well, thereby ending a two-year struggle between Michigan Oil and a variety of conservation groups. Commissioners Joan Wolfe, Carl Johnson, Harry Whiteley, and chairman Hilary Snell voted to deny the permit. The other three commissioners were absent. Said Whiteley, "After long and careful consideration, I have come to the conclusion that just because a lease is granted by the Commission, there is no obligation to grant a drilling permit [in environmentally sensitive areas]."

Carl Johnson pointed out that the Commission's decision in the Corwith well case was not simply a matter of hostility to the oil and gas industry. After all, the DNR had issued 136 drilling permits during the previous eighteen months for sites in less sensitive areas in northern Michigan. "We are trying to do right by both industry and our natural resources," he said.

Dave Smethurst hailed the victory, but he also noted that it had not come easy. The PRCA had spent $10,000 for legal help in the fight, all of it raised through small cash gifts from concerned individuals throughout Michigan, but it still had debts to the tune of $5,000.

On May 17, the DNR appointed Ford Kellum to a seventeen-member Pigeon River Country Advisory Council. There had been strong pressure from blocs within the DNR to keep him off the Council, but pressure from the public had been so overwhelming that in the end there had been little choice but to make the appointment.

Joining Kellum on the Council were Jack Hood of Interlochen (a former wildlife biologist who became the Council's chairman), Dr. Rupert Cutler (then a Michigan State University professor), various representatives of the oil and gas industry, local government officials, sportsmen, and others. All members of the Council were expected to pay their own expenses.

That summer publicity attracted hordes of sightseers to the Pigeon River Country in motor homes, four-wheel-drive and all-terrain vehicles, and motorcycles. In winter snowmobiles were everywhere. "The more desirable we attempt to make it for solitude and quiet, the more appetizing it becomes for the masses," lamented Jack Hood.

Ned Caveney also noted the problem of increasing numbers of vehicles in the forest. A college forestry student who had been hired to direct Youth Conservation Corps workers in building two hiking and cross-country ski trails through the area reported that motorcyclists were taking them over, ignoring and destroying signs. There were practically no funds to enforce the laws prohibiting such abuses.

11
TANNER DROPS
A BOMB

In August of 1974 Michigan Oil Company filed suit in Ingham County Circuit Court asking that the Natural Resources Commission's decision to impose a drilling ban be overturned. The case was expected to go all the way to the U.S. Supreme Court, and the Pigeon River Country Association was estimating that it would incur at least $50,000 in legal expenses to fight it that far. Ford Kellum issued a statewide appeal to Michigan's concerned private citizens for help.

Michigan Oil was the only company that was still seeking a free hand to drill anywhere. The rest of the oil and gas industry appeared to be going along with the DNR master plan for the Pigeon River Country. Nevertheless, there was still the problem of the twelve companies that held seventy-five percent of the leases in the forest. The major oil companies had agreed to pool their leases, but the smaller firms were at a loss to know what they should do.

Bob Strong, a DNR wildlife biologist at Gaylord, traveled to Colorado, Montana, and Wyoming at his own expense to talk to other biologists about Michigan's elk population. All of his colleagues told him that elk can tolerate the sort of intermittent disruptions created by logging operations and limited numbers of recreational vehicles, but that long-term disturbances would drive them from an area. Strong told members of the Pigeon River Country Advisory Council that the future of Michigan's elk was being made very precarious by continued oil exploration activity and poaching.

On December 13 the Natural Resources Commission appointed Dr. Howard A. Tanner to be the new director of the DNR. A former fisheries biologist, Tanner had won considerable fame as DNR fisheries chief by following through on a plan laid out by his predecessor James T. McFadden to stock the Great Lakes with Pacific salmon. Indeed, the plan was widely considered to be one of the outstanding conservation success stories of the century. Tanner had left the DNR to become a professor of natural resources at Michigan State University, and it was that position he was now leaving to return as DNR director. Kellum had some reservations about whether Tanner would be tough enough to follow through on the program that had been instituted by former DNR directors Ralph MacMullan and Gene Gazlay.

Early in 1975, Kenting Exploration Services, Ltd., of Calgary, Alberta, asked the DNR for permission to make seismic explorations of the geological formations beneath Lake Michigan, Lake Huron, and Lake Erie. Company officials stated that they were aware of the fact that Michigan law prohibited drilling in the Great Lakes, but they said that they had reason to believe that "there could be a significant change in attitude within the next two or three years" regarding offshore drilling in Lake Erie. "We have been asked by several oil companies to do the seismic work in the lakes," said Kenting officer Jack Wyder.

The best guess of the petroleum geologists was that the Niagaran Reef that extended through the Pigeon River Country and across southern Michigan near Lansing also reached out into Lake Michigan and Lake Huron, and that rich oil deposits might be found throughout the formation.

The DNR turned down Kenting's request. Natural Resouces Commission members Matt Laitala and Dean Pridgeon objected to Tanner's denial of the request, maintaining that the seismic work itself would have done no harm. Kenting stated that it would proceed with exploration work in the Canadian portion of the lakes.

In a surprise move, Governor Milliken and his wife, Helen, made a visit to the Pigeon River Country in April. Later, in a letter to Carl Johnson of the Natural Resources Commission, Mrs. Milliken wrote that "The value of wilderness deserves to be weighed with utmost care against the value of energy-producing oil. Other methods of energy production will have to be devised by mankind before the end of this century but all will concede that a vanished species cannot return again."

In a reply to Mrs. Milliken, Johnson wrote that "In our society, modern, money-dominated, it seems we must put a price on something in order to measure its worth. Resources with spiritual and aesthetic values beyond the price tend to lose out in the competition."

Along those same lines of valuation, Petoskey conservationist John Swartout did some figuring. The oil and gas industry had estimated that there were between 400 and 600 million barrels of oil under northern Lower Michigan, including the Pigeon River Country. At that point the United States was consuming oil at a rate of about 16.5 million barrels per day—and at that rate, said Swartout, all of northern Michigan's oil would be consumed in less than thirty-seven days.

In March the DNR conducted a survey of the Pigeon River Country involving twenty-four hours of aerial searching backed by 221 hours of ground searching with snowmobiles. Gaylord biologist Bob Strong released the results: there were only 159 elk spotted in the area. At most the total elk population might amount to 170 or 180. Continuing poaching was cited as the principal cause of the reduction in the herd.

On June 4, 1975, Ingham County Circuit Court Judge Thomas Brown handed down his ruling concerning the suit that Michigan Oil had brought against the DNR for refusing to grant a drilling permit for the Corwith #1-22 well site: the state of Michigan had every right to refuse permission to drill on land in the Pigeon River Country. Said Brown, "The denial of the permit to drill could validly be based partially or entirely upon ecological considerations. It is no complete answer to say that public policy demands that we develop and use our oil and gas natural resources. Wildlife and forests are also natural resources and becoming more precious, unique and unexpendable every day."

Vance Orr, the president of Michigan Oil, vowed to appeal Judge Brown's decision to the Michigan Court of Appeals. Responding to Orr's threat, Ford Kellum stated that "The fight to save the Pigeon River Country was started in 1969 and is continuing with no end in sight." He also noted that the Pigeon River Country Association had already managed to raise $20,000 to pay for their part of the necessary legal battles and that they would manage to scrape up whatever they needed to fight all the way to a final victory.

But then on August 14 the groups attempting to defend the Pigeon River Country were dealt a severe blow when DNR director Howard Tanner presented a thirty-one-page "hydrocarbon management plan," which he said laid the foundation for the DNR "to accept the challenge of orderly management of oil and gas development in the Pigeon River Country State Forest while preserving, in the long run, even enhancing, the unique surface values of the area."

The plan called for permitting drilling in the Pigeon River Country, although limiting it, at least in the beginning, to the southern third of the area, where four wells were already operating. Environmentalists had hoped that the DNR, armed with recent circuit court decisions, would block any expansion of drilling throughout the Pigeon River Country. After all, the courts had consistently ruled that the DNR could deny drilling permits regardless of whether the petitioner had purchased oil and mineral rights.

The new management plan insisted that "It has been determined that environmental disturbance and damage caused in the process, some of which is necessary and unavoidable, can be quite adequately controlled, both in degree and in specific locations."

Tanner asked that the oil companies be allowed to drill from six to twelve new wells in the general area south of the Pigeon River Country State Forest headquarters buildings. The plan called for determining the best locations for pipelines, storage and production facilities, and permanent access roads to the drilling sites only after the wells had been sunk. Commissioners voted to delay approval or denial of the Tanner plan at least until their September meeting.

Twelve days later, on August 26, Governor Milliken ordered the DNR to draft an environmental impact statement for proposed oil development in the Pigeon River Country. At the same time, the Michigan Environmental Review Board asked the DNR for an environmental impact statement to determine whether drilling should be allowed in the area at all. The Board's request did not particularly concern the oil interests, but the companies recognized that Governor Milliken's order spelled trouble for them. The drafting of an environmental impact statement and the required public hearings would effectively delay any planned drilling for months, and it would also serve to generate a lot of publicity.

Shocked by the requests for environmental impact statements from both Governor Milliken and the Environmental Review Board, Shell Oil threatened to go to court to protest the delays in drilling the studies would entail — up to eight months by its own estimates. The leases that Shell, Amoco, and Northern Michigan Exploration Company held were due to expire in 1977 and 1978, and if they hadn't begun exploratory drilling before those expiration dates, they could lose their leases.

Jerry Myers, who had succeeded Dave Smethurst as president of the Pigeon River Country Association, announced that the PRCA was exploring the possibility of suing the DNR if it adopted the Tanner plan. "Just one well, just one more, could ruin the whole forest," he said grimly.

Ford Kellum stated that he was still "absolutely opposed to any further drilling in the Pigeon River Country State Forest." He charged that Tanner and other Lansing DNR officials were trying to railroad the Pigeon River Country Advisory Council into believing there was no alternative to letting the oil companies have their way in the area.

In response to the governor's order, Tanner said that the DNR would draft an environmental impact statement "as soon as we can while doing a thorough job" — and he estimated that it would take "a month to six weeks or less, if possible." Conservation groups throughout Michigan scoffed at the idea that any statement compiled in so short a time could have any meaning.

Joe E. Stroud, editor of the *Detroit Free Press*, was quick to lambast the Tanner plan. "To many people in Michigan who watched the DNR impose a long moratorium on the granting of drilling permits and who had followed the agency's legal right to fight to be able to deny permits, the new DNR plan was a shock," Stroud wrote in an editorial. "And even more shocking, the DNR's new director, Howard Tanner, came on as an advocate of drilling.

"A vastly better solution would be to prevent any more drilling in the forest for now, even if it means a legal fight or an extension of the current leases. If it means a legal fight, Michigan ought to be prepared to take it, to preserve its right to protect even leased state land from abuse.

"Why not treat the Pigeon River oil as a reserve and leave it untouched for now? It will not go away. Its value will not diminish. Meanwhile, slant drilling techniques or other methods of extraction could well improve. The potential disruption to the forest might be further diminished.

"The chance to protect all or most of the forest was strengthened by Gov. Milliken last week. It is crucial that the issue of whether to drill at all be confronted in the next several weeks and months. The governor afforded the time. The DNR and its commission simply must use it in the public interest and provide the protection the DNR staff plan would not have afforded," Stroud concluded.

But Tanner continued to defend his unitized drilling plan, arguing that "We dare not 'lock up' the Pigeon River Country" because to wait might be to give away what were presently state-owned oil deposits to private individuals who owned parcels of land adjacent to the Pigeon River Country. He was concerned that new drilling techniques might make it possible to tap the oil under state lands with directional wells running miles diagonally. Opponents contended that Tanner was in fact presenting one of the best possible arguments to delay drilling indefinitely. Let the wells be drilled on private property, they said. Then we could get the oil without risk to the irreplaceable Pigeon River Country habitats.

Tanner also came in for some verbal lumps from the author of Michigan's Environmental Protection Act, Dr. Joseph Sax, who denounced the DNR chief's unitized drilling plan as "appalling and scandalous." And Governor Milliken reaffirmed his opposition to the Tanner plan by stating that "Just as I believe there should be no drilling on the waters of the Great Lakes, I believe steps should be taken to ban drilling in portions of Michigan's unique wilderness and other land resources.

Tanner remained adamant in advocating his proposal, however. In October he said "I have carefully reviewed the task force's evaluation of these alternatives concerning hydrocarbon exploration in the [Pigeon River Country] state forest—not to drill, or to drill in selected sections of the forest. I have chosen the alternative allowing the minimum of drilling. It appears that development in that portion of the forest would be least disruptive to the environment."

12
MUCC SUPPORTS DRILLING

DNR director Howard Tanner gained new support from an unexpected quarter on October 8, 1975, when Tom Washington, the new executive director of Michigan United Conservation Clubs, said he was convinced that the oil companies would win their five-year fight against conservationists in the end and that it was time to strike a bargain while they still had some clout. "If we can't stop them, we should seek the most palatable plan and get all the concessions we can," he said. He felt this might best be accomplished by getting Tanner to modify his basic plan for the Pigeon River Country State Forest.

MUCC's board of directors agreed with Washington when they met for their quarterly business session and moved to throw their group's support behind the Tanner plan, which called for allowing the oil industry to drill in the southern third of the 140-square-mile forest. In return for their support, they asked that the Michigan legislature earmark all of the royalties from oil and gas drilling in the Pigeon River Country to buy more land for Michigan sportsmen to use. DNR officials estimated that a total of $65 million or more would be diverted into the Game and Fish Protection Fund and that an addition $37.5 million would go into the state general fund from Pigeon River Country royalties.

A number of clubs affiliated with MUCC—including the Pigeon River Country Association, the Michigan Bear Hunters Association, and the Northland Sportsman's Club of Gaylord— were furious with the board's action. All went on record as opposing any further drilling in the Pigeon River Country State Forest. Appearing before the MUCC board, PRCA president Jerry Myers blamed "turncoat, money-hungry politicians" for putting pressure on Tanner to support drilling in the forest. Meanwhile, the 1,400 members of Canada Creek Ranch, located on 14,000 acres of land adjoining the Pigeon River Country State Forest in Montmorency County, were being wooed by the oil industry. Eager to explore under the ranch property, companies offered a $6 million lease and a twenty-five percent royalty on any gas or oil that might be discovered there.

The area was estimated to contain at least one hundred elk—possibly as much as half of all the elk left in Michigan—which roamed between the ranch country and the Pigeon River Country forest. Despite warnings from DNR biologists that noise from continuing oil activities would doom the herd, Canada Creek Ranch members voted to accept the oil companies' offer. As it turned out later, though, exploratory drilling efforts yielded only disappointing results, and the oil companies eventually abandoned the area to its original peace and quiet.

By December speculation revived about what action the Natural Resources Commission would take on the Tanner plan if the mandated environmental impact statement was acceptable. Commissioners Matt Laitala, Dean Pridgeon, and Charles Younglove were all suspected of favoring drilling. Carl T. Johnson, Hilary Snell, and Joan Wolfe were presumed to be opposed to it. Harry Whiteley, who had been on again, off again in the matter, was considered to be the swing vote.

At its December 7 meeting, the Commission reviewed the environmental impact statement that had been prepared by a DNR task force headed by Jack Bails. It suggested that drilling in the Pigeon River State Forest would have "unavoidable impacts" on the area's environment. It would adversely affect the quality of recreation the area could support, drive off the elk, and temporarily endanger some wetlands. The report recommended that if drilling was allowed at all, it should be restricted to the southern third of the forest.

"This option offers the best opportunity for compromise between extracting the majority of oil and gas, while allowing most of the forest to remain undisturbed," said Bails. "But the task force feels that even with this proposed action, the drilling will have certain unavoidable impacts. The sight, sound, and odor of oil development will adversely impact the quality, if not the quantity, of the recreational experience." The environmental impact statement suggested that disturbances could be reduced with the use of vapor control devices, noise muffling techniques, and trees and shrubs for camouflage, but it concluded that even with even with the best such efforts, the oil companies would still be making their presence quite evident in the forest: "visitors to the area will know oil and gas production is taking place," the report acknowledged.

The task force recommended that at least part of the royalties from any gas or oil production should be used to purchase additional private holdings to add to the state forest lands and for other recreational development. Public hearings to gather additional comments on the seventy-seven-page environmental impact statement were scheduled for Gaylord and Ann Arbor.

At the Gaylord hearing, which was held on December 18, representatives of the MUCC and the Michigan State Chamber of Commerce joined ranks with the oil companies to advocate drilling in the Pigeon River Country as specified in the Tanner plan.

MUCC's Tom Washington announced that "you have found black gold and it has great value. Royalties can and must be the mitigating factor which makes environmental disruption profitable. We agree that drilling may preclude elk from using parts of the area for the life of the project," he said—the DNR had estimated that the oil companies would be in the area for about twenty-five years, from 1975 to the end of the century. "We are not, however, enamored with this species and do not feel this will be an irreplaceable loss to the state if, in fact, a total loss will occur."

Ford Kellum, who had recently moved back to Traverse City after his retirement from the DNR, had a few things to say in response to Washington's statement. "All of the other natural resources that are in the Pigeon River Country now—that would be sacrificed if more oil development were allowed—are more valuable to the people of Michigan than the oil and gas that is there," he said. "Do we always have to be victims of the almighty dollar, no matter what happens to the countryside?"

Oil industry officials claimed that there might be as much as $1 billion worth of oil and gas under the Pigeon River Country State Forest, and if that much could be pumped up, the state of Michigan could receive as much as $200 million in royalties from it.

December brought its share of setbacks for the Pigeon River Country cause. For one thing, the DNR-appointed Pigeon River

Country Advisory Council, of which Ford Kellum was a member, met and voted nine to two to approve the recommendations of the DNR's environmental impact study for limited, unitized drilling in the southern third of the forest. Noting that the council had voted approval "with reluctance," chairman Dave Smethurst stated that "The environmental impact statement clearly defines the trade-offs that will occur with additional drilling. This endorsement does not imply that the council feels the environmental impact statement is without fault or that the guidelines presented are all that is needed."

Kellum continued to press his arguments, and in time the council's reluctance to approve the DNR study grew into outright opposition. At a meeting on February 7, 1976, the council reversed its December stand, voting nine to two to oppose all further drilling in the Pigeon River Country State Forest.

A similar story unfolded when the executive committee of the Michigan Chapter of the Sierra Club met on December 31, 1975. That body also voted to endorse the DNR proposal to allow limited drilling in the Pigeon River Country as a compromise move to make the best of a bad situation. Less than a month later, on January 22, furious Sierra Club members denounced the executive committee's action in a noisy four-hour meeting. As a result, the committee reversed its decision, concluding with the statement "We therefore oppose drilling in the Pigeon River Country State Forest and other wild and sensitive areas."

As 1976 began, the DNR's controversial environmental impact statement continued to generate angry words and charges from one end of the state to the other. MUCC came under particularly heavy fire from many of its own members. Tom Washington's statement that the complete loss of the Pigeon River Country's elk herd "would not be an irreplaceable loss to the state" was especially galling to conservationists and state wildlife biologists.

Howard Tanner went to the annual meeting of the Michigan Bear Hunters Association in January to try to sell his plan for the Pigeon River Country and got nowhere. The group voted unanimously to oppose all further drilling in the area. Moreover, they went on record as stating that they had "watched with dismay as other organizations, all of which are conservation-oriented and dedicated to protection of our natural resources, have one by one wavered or completely capitulated to pressures of so-called progress, which would eventually mean the gradual degradation of the Pigeon River Country."

Joseph Sax also continued to speak out on the issue, stating that the DNR's environmental impact statement was "either designed to deceive the public or . . . drafted by the DNR in ignorance of the legal situation. The only way the DNR can honestly give assurances of drilling limitations in the rest of the forest is to obtain the surrender of all leases (both public and private)."

One Michigan State University scientist, an authority on trout stream ecology, stated that "The environmental impact statement contains so little information that it cannot serve as a basis for sound decisions about oil and gas exploitation." Indeed, he stated that it was so technically inadequate that it did not even deserve to be called an environmental impact statement.

During his annual State of the State address in January, Governor Milliken asked the Michigan legislature to establish a "Heritage Trust Fund" with funds from oil and gas leases and royalties from wells drilled on state lands. According to William Rusten, Milliken's chief advisor on environmental affairs, those funds were expected to total from $9 million to $17 million in 1976, and royalties from wells in the Pigeon River Country State Forest alone were expected to amount to more than $100 million between 1976 and the year 2000.

13

THE OIL BATTLE RAGES ON

In mid-February of 1976, a panel of officers from Michigan's nineteen state agencies fought to a deadlock on an environmental assessment of a plan to allow oil and gas drilling in the Pigeon River Country State Forest. The panel sent the DNR's environmental impact statement on to the Michigan Environmental Review Board without ruling whether it adequately dealt with the question of oil drilling in the forest.

Ted Pfister, a lawyer who served as a lobbyist for Shell Oil in Lansing, told a *Detroit Free Press* reporter in March that he believed the DNR would eventually allow oil drilling in all parts of the Pigeon River Country. Once drilling got underway in the southern third of the forest, he said, the DNR was planning to study oil company operations and then draw up regulations for drilling in other, more environmentally sensitive areas. DNR officials hotly denied Pfister's remarks.

At the same time, it was revealed that back in 1974 the DNR had given Getty Oil an unpublicized extension of its lease rights to 5,480 acres in the northern part of the Pigeon River Country State Forest in which Tanner had insisted oil drilling would always be banned.

Michigan Out-of-Doors, the official publication of Michigan United Conservation Clubs, printed an article by staff member Dennis Fijalkowski that scoffed at the importance of Michigan's elk herd. The article drew a quick response from the Committee on Elk of the Pigeon River Country Advisory Council. Ford Kellum spelled out the committee's views as follows:

Fall finds bull elk bugling in the Pigeon River Country prior to breeding.
PHOTO COURTESY OF MICHIGAN TOURIST COUNCIL

"Elk are important to the Pigeon River Country concept because they are the most attractive big game animal in Michigan. Just to know there are some elk here is very important. They are a real attraction to visitors. Deer are an attraction, too, but can be seen in every county of Michigan. To see an elk in the wild is something a visitor will always remember; it could be the introduction to concern for other conservation matters.

"Elk should be a part of the 'Living Resources' program. If we should lose our elk, the Pigeon River Country would lose its most glamorous feature and much of the present attraction would be lost.

"Arguments that elk are not native to Michigan are invalid. They are here now, as are ringnecked pheasants. Both were introduced to Michigan in 1918 and all hell would break loose if we should lose either. A thought: Just what is a native plant, fish or wildlife? Very few. We have them, they are valuable, our duty is to manage them with our best knowledge for future generations.

"The ultimate goal of elk management should be to stabilize the herd at around 600 animals. Too many would cause bad effects on other animals, plants and damage farm crops as the herd did in the 1950s when the population reached 1,500 to 2,000. To occasionally see an elk is enough; too may would not be as attractive.

"Widespread habitat manipulation will not be necessary. All that is necessary to perpetuate the elk here is to provide secluded, quiet areas and adequate law enforcement with normal forest management practices and an occasional deer or elk yard cutting in an emergency caused by hard winters. Elk are grazers first and browsers second (the opposite of deer) and elk can create and maintain their own range."

Governor Milliken continued to get heavy loads of mail from concerned citizens, most of whom were opposed to further drilling in the Pigeon River Country State Forest. Among the most impressive things he received was a petition containing 30,000 signatures from people in all parts of the state urging him to do everything possible to keep the oil companies out of the Pigeon River Country.

The drive to get signatures on the petition was begun by members of the Walter Hastings Audubon Club of Traverse City, in conjuction with the Pigeon River Country Association. "Sam" Titus, secretary-treasurer of the PRCA, reported that Michigan State University wildlife management student Kenneth Case managed to collect about 10,000 signatures in the Gaylord area. The Audubon group and the PRCA gathered another 5,000 from a variety of places, including 655 from Bay City high school students and 80 from Michigan residents wintering in Waco, Texas!

At the same time, Roger Connor, a young attorney who was serving as director of the West Michigan Environmental Action Council of Grand Rapids, was asking that the DNR rewrite its environmental impact statement. "The issue here is whether there is anyplace in the state where we will say No to oil drilling," he said, "or, if I can put it in a crass way, 'Is Michigan good to the last drop?' "

On the other side of the battle lines, the Michigan Oil and Gas Association, a group representing 550 individuals and firms involved in petroleum exploration, drilling, production, refining, and transportation, stated that any further delay in approval of the existing environmental impact statement would result in a well-by-well court fight.

Carl T. Johnson of the Natural Resources Commission issued a written statement saying that he believed the oil industry

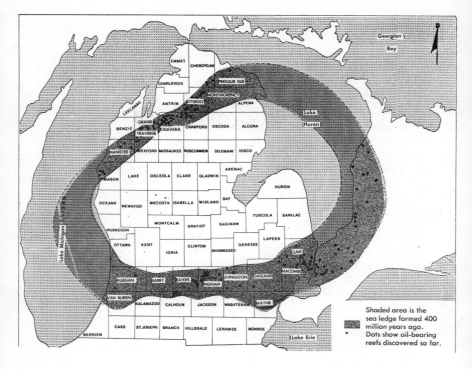

Shaded area is the
sea ledge formed 400
million years ago.
Dots show oil-bearing
reefs discovered so far.

should "quit nibbling on the edge of the Niagaran doughnut" and start taking some healthy bites from it in other parts of Michigan. He argued that the oil deposits beneath the Pigeon River Country should be left untapped as a reserve in case of a national emergency. If drilling were allowed there, he said, "I believe the next target will be Lakes Michigan and Huron."

DNR chief Tanner was also having some unforeseen problems. Rumbles of discontent were building within the department, and pressure to oust him from his office was increasing. Charges were being made that he was indecisive and secretive, and that he had withdrawn from his staff and in general isolated himself from DNR operations.

There were also less subtle charges that Tanner was making decisions in order to satisfy political factions rather than to serve the best interests of the state and its natural resources. He was accused of "fumbling the Pigeon River Country forest issue" and of trying to avoid controversy by pushing his plan through the Natural Resources Commission.

Seven professors from the University of Michigan formally criticized Tanner's plan for the Pigeon River Country in a letter to Governor Milliken. Pointing to the rape of northern Michigan forests in the late nineteenth and early twentieth centuries, the scientists noted that the region "is just now starting to extract itself [from the] environmentally insensitive resource exploitation which occurred when few knew better." They went on to argue that to allow oil and gas drilling in the Pigeon River Country would be to invite a repetition of environmental disaster in northern Michigan.

The professors stated that the oil companies had yet to demonstrate that the need for the oil and gas under the forest outweighed the environmental damage the drilling would cause. They noted in addition that any decision in the Pigeon River Country case would "bear significantly on future proposals for resource development" on other state-owned lands. "We tend to forget the relatively clean waters and young (but poor) forests of northern Michigan are but a shadow of what they might have been if given proper environmental management."

The letter was signed by William F. Benninghoff, curator of the University of Michigan ecological collection; Edward G. Boss, curator of the University of Michigan vascular plants collection; S. Ross Tocher, parks management expert; David Gates, director of the University of Michigan biological station at Pellston; Dale R. McCullough, professor of wildlife management; Jonathan W. Bulkley, associate professor of civil and water resources engineering; and Richard N. L. Andrews, associate professor of resource policy and administration.

On May 10, 1976, Governor Milliken came out strongly against oil drilling in the Pigeon River Country State Forest. He stated that he also opposed any lease extensions for the oil companies that did not contain "no-drill" clauses.

Four days later, the Natural Resources Commission, going directly against the governor's wishes, approved drilling in the Pigeon River Country in principle without specifying when, where, or how much drilling could take place. It left all those specific matters to be decided by negotiations between Tanner, the oil companies holding leases on forest lands, and the state attorney general's office.

Although the Commission's decision approved what it termed "environmentally acceptable" drilling, however, it did so only grudgingly. It officially went on record as being strongly opposed to drilling. Matt Laitala cast the only vote opposing the strongly worded statement. (Hilary Snell and Dean Pridgeon abstained on the grounds of a possible conflict of interest.) Laitala complained that the statement was just an unnecessary sop to conservationists: "We are doing this in the name of our favorite recreational pursuit, hunting, or in the name of those mangy elk that we could replace by the truckload from elk populations in the west," he said.

Ford Kellum was unhappy with the commission's action for other reasons. Commenting on the vote, which was seen as the climax of a six-year battle, he dismissed as a case of "passing the buck." He vowed to keep on fighting.

14
CITIZENS GO
TO COURT

On May 21, 1976, Shell Oil, Amoco, and Northern Michigan Exploration (Consumers Power Company) filed applications with the DNR for permits to do exploratory drilling in the Pigeon River Country State Forest. They said that they would continue to negotiate with DNR chief Howard Tanner to determine how much drilling would be allowed.

Ted Pfister, spokesman for the companies, said that they had expected "firm action" from the Natural Resources Commission but had been disappointed. "They skirted the issue and adopted a policy that was vague and seemed to continue the delays," he complained. As a result, he said, "We must begin at this time to file for drilling permits. We are confident that these energy sources so vital to a state that imports ninety percent of its energy needs can be developed with minimal impact on the forest environment."

Six days later a gas well being drilled by North American Drilling Company ten miles south of Gaylord exploded. Burning out of control, the blown out well was releasing 300,000 cubic feet of natural gas per hour and producing flames that shot 400 feet into the air. As had been the case with a similar Michigan oil well fire in 1970, it took the expertise of oil well fire fighter Red Adair to subdue the inferno and recap the well. It was three weeks before he could finish the job. The whole episode was causing a lot of second thoughts among those who had come out in favor of drilling in the Pigeon River Country.

Meeting at Sault Ste. Marie on June 11, the Natural Resources Commission approved a "compromise" plan that would allow drilling in 15,000 acres of the southern third of the Pigeon River Country State Forest. The plan also called for a moratorium on all drilling in some northern sectors of the forest for as many as ten years and for extending other leases on northern lands for twenty-five years with nondevelopment stipulations. Matt Laitala, Harry Whiteley, and Joan Wolfe voted for the drilling plan; Carl T. Johnson cast the only No vote.

Governor Milliken registered his disappointment with the Commission's plan, stating that he would have preferred an outright ban on drilling. The Commission responded that it had been advised by the attorney general's office that such a ban could not have been legally enforced, and that the best way to maintain some control over drilling was to give the oil companies some of what they wanted in the way of drilling permits. "Clearly, the state of Michigan made an error in 1968 in leasing the Pigeon River Country for oil development," said Milliken.

Bitterly disppointed by the Commission's action, Ford Kellum noted publicly that in a television interview once, Tanner had promised that he would be guided by the peoples' wishes in fulfilling his task for the DNR. "He has not and he should resign," said Kellum. The retired biologist also said that he felt the Commission had shirked its responsibility and that except for Carl Johnson it "should be replaced by knowledgeable people who would not be so easily influenced by big industry and who could say No when it was the right answer."

"Piece by piece, land developers and big oil companies get their way with the state and federal government," Kellum continued. "Our most valuable recreational, forest, and agricultural lands are being lost for future generations."

Still stubbornly determined, Kellum and his son, Blaine, put together an "Environmental Communications Service" later in June. Its purpose was to "promote the general welfare of the people by encouraging, through communications, a collective voice of the citizenry in multiple-use and management of the environment and the natural resources." The men viewed the new service as "an early warning system for the environment."

That same month, officials in the attorney general's office denied that they had told Tanner to accept the oil company plans as the best he could legally obtain to protect the Pigeon River Country.

Assistant attorneys general Charles Alpert and Stewart Freeman, who had been assigned to work with Tanner during negotiations with the oil industry, said that he had not consulted them about the advisability of seeking any concessions from the companies. In fact Alpert said that both he and Freeman had told Tanner that they believed the courts would support a DNR refusal to permit drilling on a well-by-well basis if there were evidence to indicate that drilling would be likely to cause environmental damage. Such a ruling was upheld by the Ingham County Circuit Court, and a similar case was pending in the Michigan Court of Appeals at the time.

Spokesmen for the Pigeon River Country Association said that they might seek a motion to get the Natural Resources Commission to reconsider its decision to allow drilling. Lawyers had informed them that the Commission's action had been illegal because it had made its decision without having given public notice or the opportunity for any sort of public involvement. Attorney Roger Connor told members of the PRCA that it could legally request the Commission to delay implementation of its order until the public had had a chance to examine and comment on it.

On August 13, 1976, the Natural Resources Commission refused a formal request that it review its June decision to allow drilling in the forest. The Pigeon River Country Association, the West Michigan Environment Action Council, Trout Unlimited, the Sierra Club, and the Michigan Nature Association all vowed to challenge the Commission's decision in Ingham County Circuit Court on the grounds that its agreement with the oil companies was illegal and ignored provisions of both the Michigan Environmental Protection Act and the state's Oil and Gas Act.

Meanwhile, Tanner ordered DNR field biologists and foresters to inspect those areas in the Pigeon River Country State Forest that the oil companies were seeking to develop as drilling sites and make recommendations about where drilling would produce the least environmental damage. The field men refused to approve any of the sites, including one on which an oil company marking stake had been kicked over by an elk.

The issue of oil drilling in the Great Lakes came up again in August as well. The Great Lakes Basin Commission, a group composed of representatives from state and federal agencies, recommended that Lake Michigan and Lake Huron be explored for possible oil and gas deposits. The recommendation stirred up another hornet's nest of opposition from the groups fighting for the protection of the Pigeon River Country.

Among those blasting the idea was Joe Stroud, editor of the

Detroit Free Press, who asked in an editorial, "Is anyone so naive as to think that an industry that has fought so doggedly for the right to drill in the scenic Pigeon River Country State Forest — which also sits astride the oil-and-gas-rich Niagaran Reef—would be willing to stop at the water's edge, if there were any chance of offshore drilling?"

Stroud stated that the federal agencies should be given the message that "The quality of Michigan offshore waters is not for sale. The submerged lands belong to the public and their management will continue to be in the public interest, not in the interest of the gas and oil industry."

In June, July, and again in August, the Natural Resources Commission refused requests to withdraw its decision to go along with the Tanner drilling plan until it could be reviewed by the public. In the end, the coalition of conservation groups dedicated to protecting the Pigeon River Country had no choice but to take legal action. In October of 1976 they filed suit in the Ingham County Circuit Court asking that the Commission's agreement with the oil companies by overturned.

At the judge's request, the DNR agreed to issue no drilling permits until a show-cause hearing was held on October 28. The coalition bringing suit against the DNR grew beyond the four groups that had originally announced its intent to fight the decision. The new volunteers included the Detroit and Thunder Bay Audubon Clubs, Northland Sportsman's Club of Gaylord, the Michigan Student Environmental Confederation, and the Michigan Lakes and Streams Association.

Environmental attorneys Roger Connor and Dr. Joseph Sax cited what they considered to be legal authority to keep drilling rigs, pipelines, storage facilities, trucks, and new roads out of the Pigeon River Country forest. They contended that the actions of the Natural Resources Commission and the DNR violated both the Michigan Environmental Protection Act and the Michigan Constitution of 1921 that created protective agencies. Connor said that he expected the oil companies to enter the suit on the DNR's side.

In a separate court case, the Michigan Court of Appeals ruled on October 21 to uphold the DNR's refusal to grant drilling rights to Michigan Oil Company. The court warned, however, that the DNR would find it difficult to block future permits unless it drew up a comprehensive forest management program that spelled out clear policies regarding the disposition of mineral rights on state lands. Connor was elated at the decision.

Michigan Oil said it would appeal the decision to the Michigan Supreme Court.

Eight days later, Connor found himself in Ingham County Circuit Court battling the DNR and its Commission. On November 9, Judge Thomas Brown handed down a decision. Although he declined to issue a blanket ban on drilling in the Pigeon River Country State Forest, he did rule that the Commission's agreement with the oil companies did not in itself authorize drilling. He held that all drilling permits would have to be subject to further review to prove that drilling would not cause any environmental damage, and he noted that citizens would have the right to contest any permits under the provisions of the Michigan Environmental Protection Act and the Oil and Gas Act. Both Connor and the DNR considered the ruling to be a partial victory.

DNR field men continued to review proposed drilling sites. Out of ten proposed sites they managed to rule out one as being completely unsuitable.

At its December meeting, the Natural Resources Commission reviewed and then tabled an elk management plan for the Pigeon River Country. Tom Washington, the executive director of Michigan United Conservation Clubs voiced strong objections to the plan, arguing that there were "programs that would be far more important to wildlife in general than this [elk] proposal," and dismissing elk as a "high-priced luxury—one the state can ill afford."

15

ROGER CONNOR vs. BIG OIL

As 1977 began, United Geophysical Company went ahead and conducted seismic tests in the northern portion of the Pigeon River Country State Forest for oil companies holding leases there, despite at least two DNR refusals to allow such testing. The area had clearly been designated no-drill territory under the Tanner plan. The infraction of DNR rules was revealed by Northern Michigan Exploration Company (Consumers Power), which said that "appropriate action" would be taken against the offender — although it was never specified what that action would have been.

Dr. Rupert M. Cutler, a close personal friend of Ford Kellum and a longtime member of the Pigeon River Country Advisory Council, left Michigan early in 1977 to become Assistant U.S. Secretary of Agriculture for Conservation, Research, and Education. (He later went on to mastermind the RARE II program for the national forests.) The groups working to protect the Pigeon River Country were going to miss his valuable advice, born of a healthy impatience with "bumbling bureaucrats" and a wealth of experience from a distinguished career in conservation that included work for the U.S. Forest Service, National Audubon Society, Virginia Commission of Game and Inland Fisheries, National Wildlife Federation, and Michigan State University School of Natural Resources. Nevertheless, the fight went on.

Despite strong objections from its field men, the DNR issued a drilling permit on February 8 for a site that was located

300 feet from the edge of a swamp, 500 feet from a creek that drained into Canada Creek, and less than a mile and a half from the boundary of the Pigeon River Country forest. DNR officials later admitted that they had made a mistake in issuing the permit — DNR policy clearly prohibited drilling within a quarter-mile of any watercourse — but they had failed to notice the small streams designated on the maps. They said it wouldn't happen again.

The DNR held a public meeting in Lansing on February 28 to help decide whether to grant nine proposed drilling permits in the Pigeon River Country forest. Comments made by the audience of about 250 in attendance were taped for the record. Most of those who testified voiced opposition to all drilling. Ford Kellum submitted written testimony based on personal on-site inspections that indicated drilling at all of the sites selected by Shell Oil would do irreparable harm to environmental features.

Field men from the Gaylord DNR district also spoke up in opposition to development of some of the sites. Steve Swan, a fisheries biologist, gave evidence suggesting that at least five of the sites should be restricted. Other witnesses noted that Shell was proposing to drill at multiple sites to avoid more costly slant drilling even though half-mile directional wells were feasible in the area. In addition, most of the proposed sites were distant from existing roads; to provide access to the new wells, "closed trails" would have to be widened and improved for truck traffic if the permits were approved.

On April 13, Tanner agreed to give the groups opposed to the drilling an opportunity to submit written testimony concerning development plans for the area. He promised that he would make a decision based on the written testimony and the taped interviews from the February hearing no later than November 1, 1977. But then two weeks later representatives of Shell Oil, Amoco, and Consumers Power asked the Ingham County Circuit Court to block further hearings on the grounds that they would "serve no useful purpose." The oil firms expected a court hearing on the matter by June.

On May 6, the Michigan Supreme Court announced its refusal to overturn lower court rulings blocking Michigan Oil Company from drilling in the Pigeon River Country State Forest. Attorneys for the company acknowledged that the Supreme Court's refusal to hear an appeal motion probably meant an end to the so-called "Corwith #1-22 Case," widely considered to be a landmark case in the battle between the oil companies and opponents of drilling. Attorney General Frank Kelley said that he was "very satisfied" with the decision.

The ruling left in force a Michigan Court of Appeals ruling that stated "Clearly the lease does not guarantee that the lessee will be permitted to drill for oil. The commission expressly retained its statutory authority to fulfill its duty to the people of the State of Michigan by regulating the use of the state lands and resources placed in its control and held by them as a public trust." Which is to say that if the DNR determined that drilling was likely to cause what it considered to be unacceptable environmental damage, it had every right to reject applications for permission to drill. In effect, it opened to way for the DNR to return to a no-drill option for the whole Pigeon River Country State Forest.

In June attorney Roger Connor urged the Natural Resources Commission to oppose further drilling in the Pigeon River Country. He noted that the Commission had come to its agreement with Shell Oil while it was under the impression that it had no legal authority to block drilling, but that the Supreme Court ruling had demonstrated that that was not the case. Connor also pointed out that the commissioners had been led to believe that drilling would be conducted at sites along existing roads, whereas the sites in question were actually located in largely undeveloped areas. And finally, Connor argued that the testimony indicating that the southern third of the Pigeon River Country was the least fragile section of the forest was in error: the lands actually contained the most wetlands and were the source of two major rivers. Tanner promised to make recommendations to the Commission in August.

On August 24, Tanner formally approved all ten of Shell's applications to drill exploratory wells in the Pigeon River Country forest. "I have made the determination, in accepting my staff's recommendation to approve these applications, that there will be no unnecessary waste in the forest as a result of drilling, no pollution, impairment, or destruction," he said, "and that the most reasonable and prudent locations for the drilling sites have been selected."

The same week, Ingham County Circuit Court Judge Michael Harrison issued a temporary restraining order prohibiting Shell from preparing drilling sites for oil and gas exploration in the Pigeon River Country. The ruling came in response to a request that had been submitted by Roger Connor and the ten groups he was representing after the DNR had refused their appeal on the matter. In issuing the restraining order, Harrison noted "We are balancing here minimal financial loss on the standpoint of the defendants [Shell] against very obvious irreparable harm [to the forest]."

On September 6, Ingham County Circuit Court Judge Thomas Brown refused to grant a request for a preliminary injunction against drilling in the Pigeon River Country forest, although he did agree to grant time for an appeal of his decision by issuing a stay that effectively prevented the oil companies from beginning work in the area while Connor filed his appeal with the Michigan Court of Appeals.

On September 21 the Appeals Court said in effect that since there was a DNR administrative moratorium on drilling until November 30 because of the elk breeding season, it would not do any harm to hold up drilling for a hearing in the meantime. It ruled that a trial to be presided over by Judge Brown should be held on or before October 10 to decide the matter.

Connor filed suit against the DNR, Howard Tanner, Shell Oil Company, Amoco, and Northern Michigan Exploration Company. On October 11 he faced off against state assistant attorney general Stewart Freeman and a battery of attorneys representing the oil companies at a trial held in Mason, Michigan.

Six days later, Judge Brown, who had never been in the Pigeon River Country, visited the area and was impressed with what he saw.

When the trial resumed on October 18, Connor called an independent geologist, a noise expert, and a hydrologist as witnesses. The geologist testified that DNR estimates of oil reserves under the Pigeon River Country were as much as sixty-six percent too high, and that even if all of the oil were successfully removed it wouldn't make a dent in the country's overall needs. The noise expert testified that the planned oil field would generate noise that would be audible from one to three miles from the drilling site, depending on its location. The hydrologist testified that inevitable oil spills would contaminate both groundwater and streams.

Subsequent witnesses included Ford Kellum, who noted that the DNR had leased mineral rights to the oil companies without having consulted its field men and that development would adversely affect elk and other wildlife.

Dr. James W. Hall, a Traverse City physician who regularly fished the Black River and enjoyed the solitude of the area, testified that oil facilities would destroy it and drive him away.

Fisheries biologist Steve Swan said that the Black River was the longest brook trout stream left in the lower peninsula and that pipeline crossings would pollute it with sediment no matter how well they were regulated by the DNR.

Forester Ned Caveney noted that the southern portion of the Pigeon River Country was a quiet, rustic area and one of the few spots left in Michigan where people could escape from the noise of machinery, vehicles, and other people.

Several individuals contributed testimony on the quality of hunting in the Pigeon River Country, including Carl Johnson of the Natural Resources Commission, Doug Mummert, and Don Edgerton.

By December 2, Shell Oil was so confident that the trial was going in its favor that it began clearing operations at six of the ten proposed sites in the forest. It held off on work at the remaining four sites, about which the judge had expressed some doubt. Three days later, Judge Brown ruled against Connor, who immediately asked for forty-eight hours to take the case to the Court of Appeals. Brown allowed the site clearing to proceed.

On December 13, the Appeals Court denied Connor's request for an order to halt drilling in the Pigeon River Country, but it agreed to review the lower court decision that upheld the state's actions in granting Shell permission to drill ten exploratory wells in keeping with the agreement settled on June 11, 1976. The court also gave Connor until February 1, 1978, to file briefs explaining his position and said that it would act on them in April of that year. Connor raised the possibility of petitioning the state's Supreme Court to temporarily block expanded drilling in the Pigeon River Country, but it looked like a forlorn hope for the Pigeon River Country Association and the other opponents of drilling he was representing.

By December 15, Shell Oil drilling crews had penetrated to the 3,000-foot level in the first well being sunk toward the Niagaran Reef.

On December 22, the Michigan Supreme Court acted on an emergency appeal from Connor and ordered Shell Oil not to clear any new sites or sink any new wells in the Pigeon River Country. It was a small victory—drilling was going to have to be suspended from April 15 to July 15 in accordance with DNR regulations designed to protect the elk herd during the critical calving season anyway—but it served to give Connor, Kellum, and many others a slightly more optimistic Christmas.

On December 28, Shell decided to cap the Charlton #111

well in the Pigeon River Country. The company removed the drilling rig and cleared out other equipment for the winter. The company's lawyers said they'd have to wait for the outcome of drilling injunction and the results of an ecological suit that had been filed by the West Michigan Environmental Action Council, the Pigeon River Country Association, and other allied groups.

16

SUPREME COURT DECISION

On January 6, 1978, the Michigan Supreme Court agreed to hear the case against exploration for oil in the Pigeon River Country State Forest even though it was still pending before the state's Court of Appeals. The December 22 injunction to keep Shell Oil Company from clearing any new sites in the forest was kept in effect. The Supreme Court action effectively removed the case from the hands of the Court of Appeals and gave some promise of a quicker resolution of the long dispute.

Survey results released on January 7 showed that the elk population was up from 159 sighted the previous year to 255. The increase was attributed to more effective prevention of poaching and an increase in quiet areas following restrictions of oil and gas exploration activities.

Roger Connor and other consulting environmental attorneys believed that the high court would not have taken over the Pigeon River Country suit if it had not been sympathetic toward the effort to prevent the area from becoming an oil field. The court took over the case only days after Justice G. Mennen Williams had made a widely quoted speech on the significance of the Michigan Environmental Protection Act and the need to uphold it. Pigeon River Country Association members and Connor had long charged that Tanner had violated the MEPA when he and the Natural Resources Commission had authorized drilling in the Pigeon River Country.

Holding that the Pigeon River Country case and the Corwith #1-22 case were similar, the Supreme Court directed that they be tried together. In the Corwith case, the DNR was defending its refusal to allow Michigan Oil Company to drill on the Round Lake Trail in the southern Pigeon River Country forest. In the Pigeon River Country case, the DNR was saying that drilling as many as fifty wells in the southern third of the forest would not damage the environment. Connor argued that the DNR positions in the two suits contradicted each other. More than a year would pass before the court handed down its decision.

During the long wait for the high court ruling, DNR director Howard Tanner offered Ford Kellum a reappointment to his seat on the Pigeon River Advisory Council for a term that would run through June 30, 1981. Kellum turned him down, charging that the meetings of the citizen council were being so overpowered by representatives from the Roscommon and Lansing offices of the DNR, all trying to persuade the council members to their way of thinking, that the group had for all intents and purposes outlived it usefulness. Kellum pointed proudly to the Pigeon River Country Association as a group that had a "much bigger clout than does the advisory council."

Finally, on February 20, 1979, the Michigan Supreme Court ruled by a four-to-three majority that the consortium of oil developers could not drill its ten proposed exploratory wells in the Pigeon River Country State Forest because of the environmental damage it would cause. Those rendering the majority opinion were Blair Moody, Jr.; John W. Fitzgerald; James L. Ryan; and G. Mennen Williams.

"Unquantifiable damage that will result from drilling of the ten exploratory wells" was cited in concluding that the conduct of the defendants (Shell Oil and the DNR) would constitute an impairment or destruction of a natural resource.

In the related Corwith #1-22 case, the high court ruled by a similar four-justice majority during the same month that the Natural Resources Commission had acted within its legal authority in denying Michigan Oil Company a permit to drill for oil in the Pigeon River Country forest. The court held that state laws enacted in 1921 and 1939 granted the DNR the power to deny drilling permits in any cases in which the Pigeon River Country's unique wilderness environment would be threatened by the development. Dissenting justices said that the case should have been tried under the more recent Michigan Environmental Protection Act and chided the DNR for having failed to raise the MEPA as an issue in the long-fought Corwith case.

The twin rulings had the effect of prohibiting oil and gas

drilling throughout the entire Pigeon River Country State Forest. The court also ruled that the DNR was not obligated to extend expired oil company leases.

State foresters announced that they would give immediate priority to the preparation of a complete management plan for the Pigeon River Country forest, a job that had been held up during the court proceedings. The new plan was to call for continued concentration on wildlife and timber management and better controls on recreational activities in the area, including restrictions on mechanized travel in certain parts of the forest.

Stung by the defeat, the oil industry protested that the nation's energy needs made it important to develop all available sources. Connor scoffed at their claims, pointing out the fact that only three percent of the Niagaran Reef deposits in northern Michigan were located under the Pigeon River Country and that the oil companies would still have access to the other ninety-seven percent.

As great as Connor's pleasure was at the outcome of his very first court case, it would not begin to compare with what Ford Kellum was feeling. Congratulations poured in to him from every part of Michigan and many other states as well, both by telephone and mail.

Helen Milliken, wife of the governor, wrote to say "I thought of you when the recent Supreme Court Pigeon River decision was reached. It was a vindication of a long and sometimes lonely battle which you waged. There may be no published plaudits for your perseverance and dedication but I am sure the satisfaction is one that deeply warms the heart. You performed a great service for all of us."

On March 16, Tanner informed oil company representatives that the DNR would not go along with them in seeking a rehearing of the high court decision banning drilling in the Pigeon River Country State Forest. Two months later the Michigan Supreme Court denied Shell Oil's request for a rehearing.

*   *   *

Basking in the glow of victory, members and friends of the Pigeon River Country Association gathered in Grayling on June 23, 1979, to celebrate. Their jubilation was tempered with the realization that future battles might still have to be fought, though.

Dave Smethurst, the first president of the Association, served as emcee for the meeting. "This sure has been an emotional thing to me," he said, "and I'm sure it has been an important part of all your lives, too." He cited the many who had aided the effort during the nearly decade-long fight and then singled out a few who had "gone beyond the call of duty," along with many media sources "without whose help the whole thing might have gone down the tube."

"I wanted to present the Cow Pie Award to Howard Tanner and [other DNR officials], but we're not going to do that," he chuckled. "My wife wouldn't let me bake them in the oven!"

Instead, he presented Ford Kellem with the first PRCA Award, recalling the biologist's early declaration that "We won't give up, because if we're right, we'll win!" The award, a life-size carving of the now-extinct passenger pigeon, reminded the audience of how close the "Big Wild" status of the Pigeon River Country had come to extinction.

Similar awards went to environmental attorneys Roger Connor and Gary Rentrop, who had volunteered countless hours in helping to win the victory. Other recipients included Dr. Sibley Hoobler, the *Detroit Free Press*, Glen Sheppard and *The North Woods Call*, Jerry Myers, Carl T. Johnson (the only member of the Natural Resources Commission "who stood firm right from the start"), Pigeon River Country Association secretary-treasurer "Sam" Titus, and Dr. Joseph L. Sax.

Sax, the University of Michigan law professor who wrote the Michigan Environmental Protection Act and worked closely with attorneys on the Pigeon River Country case, recapped the events that had led to the fight and the part the state's Environmental Protection Act had played in securing the victory:

"Lawsuits over environmental issues are always a matter of last resort. They are a kind of desperation strategy. When those who are supposed to administer the law—in this case, the Department of Natural Resources and the Natural Resources Commission—do not do the job that they ought to do, when other institutions in the society, like the press, the governor's office, or citizen expressions of opinion, however strong and well-meaning, are unable to bring about much-needed change, then with great reluctance we as citizens have no choice but to go to court. It's because ultimately the source of vitality in the community, the source of vindication of environmental rights, lies in the grass roots people in the state that this whole enterprise known as the Pigeon River controversy got started.

"This was a hard case. It was a hard case legally, and it was an extremely difficult case politically. In the nine years since the law has been on the books, there has been no more important case that has invoked the Environmental Protection Act. This is the biggest single case that has utilized the statute since it was first enacted. It is a big-money case, and big-money cases mean big power. There are two big powers involved in this case. One, of course, is the oil companies. And the oil companies, as people who work not only on the local but on the national and international scene, have more money, more expertise, more employees, more political muscle and influence than any other industry in the country.

"The other major power, I'm sorry to say, on the wrong side of this case was the Department of Natural Resources and the Natural Resources Commission. Unfortunately, every effort to persuade the DNR and NRC to make the right decision only pushed them further and further into a corner. They persuaded themselves not only that they made the right decision, but that they ought to fight as hard as they could to sustain that decision. And they did that.

"This case is important because it demonstrates something that needs to be demonstrated over and over and over again: ordinary citizens, people without a lot of expertise, without a lot of political influence, who scrimp and save for every dollar (and there were a lot of dollars scrimped for in this case, as all of you well know) can win despite enormous odds if they have the determination, the conviction that they're right, and they have the law behind them.

"The Pigeon River case is not only important as that kind of David-and-Goliath victory and because the Pigeon River substantively is worth saving, but because it now stands as part of the body of legal precedent that others will look to.

"It is important that the case got decided in 1979. This was not the first case decided by the Michigan Supreme Court upholding the validity of the Environmental Protection Act, but it's the first case in the energy crisis era in which so many people think strong commitments to environmental protection have been severely diminished.

"This was the first significant case involving the management of the state's public lands. That is important because this state has a very large quantity of state-owned public lands.

"This case was also important because of the oil and gas leases involved. A very critical legal question raised by this case was whether we had to live with those decisions made before environmental awareness rose, before we appreciated the implications of drilling in this particular area, and before the enactment of certain modern environmental laws. Do we have to accept decisions simply because they were made years ago?

"The court made clear that even though leases had been granted, modern environmental laws had to govern the application for permits to drill. That ruling, as a legal matter, is an important protection against past short-sightedness.

"I want to say something to put you on guard, because this case isn't over. As soon as the victory came down in the Supreme Court, arduously won after being in the Circuit Court and briefly in the Court of Appeals, finally getting to the Supreme Court, which people think of as the final court, you think it's all over. But it wasn't over, because the next thing that the oil company defendant did was to appeal in the Supreme Court for a rehearing, a rehashing of the whole thing.

"Fortunately, that petition for rehearing has been denied. But they're not finished yet, because now they have given notice that they are going to go to the Supreme Court of the United States and seek to reopen the litigation. I'm very hopeful and I'm confident they will not prevail in the U.S. Supreme Court.

"There will be efforts made at the administrative level and there will be efforts made at the legislative level to overturn these victories. You've got to continue to be vigilant. You should be happy, you should be pleased with yourself, you should be pleased with each other. But don't fall asleep, because there's a saying among developers — especially true as the value of the resources at stake rises — 'Money can always wait.' "

Epilog

Big oil, big money, and special interests never give up. This became only too apparent in early 1980, when the worst fears of those who loved the Pigeon River Country came to pass. The dire warnings of Dr. Joseph Sax rang true as Michigan slid into an economic recession that threatened to edge into the proportions of a full-scale depression.

Shell Oil Company attorneys and lobbyists, wooing state lawmakers with promises of easy cash to bail Michigan out of its financial woes, wrote Senate Bill 1119. It looked so simple and easy that twenty-nine of the state's thirty-six senators signed it as sponsors. SB-1119 was designed to permit drilling for oil and gas in Michigan's state parks, offshore areas of the Great Lakes, and other protected areas in the state.

Knowing that the bill would never make it out of the Senate Conservation Committee, legislative leaders managed to have it assigned to the friendlier Senate Commerce Committee, which concerns itself more with money matters than with the environment. Ironically, the bill that was designed to crucify Michigan's environment was sent to committee just prior to the Easter recess, on April 3, 1980, which left no time for opponents to head off the action.

Among the first to see through the strategy and sound the battle cry were Sax and former member of the Natural Resources Commission Carl T. Johnson. Both men called the bill "blatant special interest" legislation among a lot of other unprintable things.

"The important thing is not what it says but what it doesn't say," noted Johnson. "There is not one word in it that indicates our state parks, dedicated wilderness areas, or Great Lakes waters are to be protected from invasion by the drillers."

Sax charged that the bill "would repeal the central provisions of the Michigan Environmental Protection Act. Indeed, it would repeal all of Michigan's environmental laws—air, water, waste disposal, toxics—in regard to oil and gas activities. And, by the creation of a unique legal presumption, the bill defines routine activities of that industry as lawful under all Michigan laws."

Sax also pointed out that SB-1119 would require the DNR to prepare a plan for oil and gas development of lands that had "exceptional environmental value"—a plan that would make it "impossible to shelter even the most unique or fragile lands from development." He went on to say that "It would deny any discretion of the Natural Resources Commission to reject such a plan so long as normal oil industry practices are used."

Meanwhile, lawmakers were staunchly defending the bill, noting that lifting the drilling ban in the Pigeon River Country State Forest would bring an extra $800 million dollars into the state treasury.

"All they are interested in is making money," concluded Carl Johnson. "They don't care what happens to the land or the people who want to use it for recreation." He called on the legislature to scrap SB-1119 and instead to mandate the creation of a "Pigeon River Country Oil Reserve." He suggested that signs be posted in the area explaining "The petroleum under this forest is being stored here for future generations."

Ignoring the arguments presented by Sax, Johnson, and other concerned Michigan citizens, Tom Washington, executive director of Michigan United Conservation Clubs, began stumping the state with representatives of Shell Oil. They did their utmost at news conferences to sell the media and the Michigan citizenry on the benefits to be derived from opening the Pigeon River Country to oil and gas drilling.

When it became painfully clear that the politicians were willing to effectively repeal the Michigan Environmental Protection Act in order to get at the riches beneath in the Pigeon River Country, opposition began to crumble statewide. Even the strongest supporters of the Pigeon River Country, including the West Michigan Environmental Action Council and some members of the Pigeon River Country Association, suspected that the stakes were getting too high. If they took on the oil companies and lost this time, they might lose everything, opening the way for drilling everywhere in the state. One by one, conservation groups reluctantly concluded that a compromise was the only way left to ensure at least some environmental protection.

Proposing a compromise to members of the Pigeon River Country Association, Dave Smethurst summed things up by saying, "The bottom line is that this is the best we can do."

Ford Kellum was joined by Doug Mummert, who had been president of the PRCA for three years, in stubbornly opposing any compromise in the matter, but they were ultimately left in a dwindling minority.

Fortunately, the opponents of drilling still had a strong ally in Governor William Milliken, who threatened to veto SB-1119 unless legislators made a number of important changes in it to safeguard remaining state lands. These changes—which included restricting drilling in the Pigeon River State Forest to the southern third of the land and imposing strict environmental safeguards on all development—were eventually made. The bill was passed, and the governor signed it into law early in 1980.

On December 15, 1980, the DNR and the Natural Resources Commission agreed to abide by a decision handed down by the Ingham County Circuit Court in a suit brought against them and Shell Oil by the West Michigan Environmental Action Council. The agreement banned all exploration and drilling in the northern two-thirds of the forest for a period of twenty years and put a practical end to litigation concerning hydrocarbon development in the Pigeon River Country.

Ford Kellum was not at all happy with the decision, but he did see some good coming out of it nonetheless. "If we hadn't been on the oil companies' tails, they would have drilled that forest to pieces," he said. "It would have been like fifty years ago, when the oil companies had no regard for anything but to get the oil out. Now they wouldn't dare do that because of the bad publicity they would get. I think the fight did a heck of a lot of good!"

Early in 1981 Shell began drilling what may turn out to be some fifty wells in the area, under some of the strictest environmental standards ever imposed on any industry by any governmental agency. Of the first thirteen wells drilled, six turned out to be producers of oil or gas, although it soon became apparent that the forecasts of the riches that would accrue to the industry and the state had been greatly exaggerated.

Those who had battled so long and hard to preserve the Pigeon River Country in its pristine state still had one parting shot to deliver. Appropriately enough, it was made by Ford Kellum: according to the very best estimates of the state and the oil companies, there are at most about seventy-seven million barrels of oil and seventy-seven billion cubic feet of natural gas beneath the Pigeon River Country—which, as Kellum pointed out, is enough oil to last the United States about four days and enough gas to last about two minutes at current rates of use.

Was it all really worth it?

* * *

The people of Michigan, particularly those of future generations, owe a debt of gratitude to the many "little people" who dared do battle against overwhelming odds in order to save the Pigeon River Country. As Doug Mummert put it so well, "These little people are the true giants of the Michigan conservation movement. Without each and every one of them, the Pigeon River Country would be just another oil field today."

Apologizing to those we have missed, we still want to salute the following individuals, who come to mind for the parts they played in the epic struggle that lasted more than a decade:

Bo Abrahms	Mark Dilts
Al Beaulieu	Don Edgerton
Ed Becker	Charles Eisendrath
Dr. Tom Bell	Lee Ekstrom
Dr. Ted Black	Joe Ellis
Gary Boushelle	Henry Erb
Cliff Bragdon	Charles Evenson, Sr.
Kathy Bramer	Dave Franz
Patricia Bravender	Sandy Franz
Mr. and Mrs. Jim Bricker	Bill Fraser
Chet Briggs	Doug Fulton
Sue Briggs	Marguerite Gahagan
Ned Caveney	Liz Gall
Fr. Patrick Cawley	Geoff Gillis
Roy Chapin, Jr.	Pat Goling
Gordie Charles	Ruth Gruitch
Barb Clark	Dr. Jim Hall
Asta Conner	Mrs. Cecil Harbour
Roger Conner	Carl Heidel
Rup Cutler	Eunice Hendricks
Bertha Daubendiek	Bill Hodgins
Jeff Daupin	Dr. Sibley Hoobler
Fred Dilley	Jack Hood

Larry Hull
John Hunting
Les Iscokovich
Carl T. Johnson
Nels Johnson
Ford Kellum
Ralph King
Virgil LaPlant
Paul Leach
T. G. Lefeque
Gene Little
Al Litzenberger
Diane Lobenstahl
P. S. Lovejoy
Randy McCune
John MacGregor
John Makris
Ron May
Ed Meany
John Merkle
Ginny Meyers
Jerry Meyers
Linda Meyers
Mike Moore
Dick Moran
Betty Mummert
Doug Mummert
Pete Murdick
Janet Nave
Ross Nave
Tom Opre
Gene Oschner
Priscilla Oschner
Martha Partfet
Zyg Pater

Bill Pearson
Bob Philip
Rhett Pinsky
Archie Reeves
Doug Reeves
Jerry Rentrop
Alex Sagady
Austin Sanford
Dr. Joseph L. Sax
Edith Schultz
Reg Sharkey
Glen Sheppard
Fred Sibley
Dave Smethurst
Sue Smethurst
Carol Smith
Boyd Snider
George Snyder
Phil Soper
Bob Strong
Joe Stroud
Steve Swan
Dr. John Tanton
"Sam" Titus
Ross Tossler
Jack Van Coevereing
Rip Van Winkle
Pete Vellenga
Jack Wallig
Jim Welch
Dr. Ray White
Steve Working
Bill Yerkes
Dr. Bev Zeldt